ROUTLEDGE LIBRARY EDITIONS:
MANAGEMENT

Volume 36

THE SCIENCE OF LABOUR
AND ITS ORGANIZATION

THE SCIENCE OF LABOUR
AND ITS ORGANIZATION

JOSEFA IOTEYKO

LONDON AND NEW YORK

First published in 1919 by George Routledge & Sons, Limited

This edition first published in 2018
by Routledge
2 Park Square, Milton Park, Abingdon, Oxon OX14 4RN

and by Routledge
711 Third Avenue, New York, NY 10017

Routledge is an imprint of the Taylor & Francis Group, an informa business

British Library Cataloguing in Publication Data
A catalogue record for this book is available from the British Library

ISBN: 978-1-138-55938-7 (Set)
ISBN: 978-1-351-05538-3 (Set) (ebk)
ISBN: 978-1-138-57059-7 (Volume 36) (hbk)
ISBN: 978-0-203-70338-0 (Volume 36) (ebk)

Publisher's Note
The publisher has gone to great lengths to ensure the quality of this reprint but points out that some imperfections in the original copies may be apparent.

Disclaimer
The publisher has made every effort to trace copyright holders and would welcome correspondence from those they have been unable to trace.

The Science of Labour

AND

Its Organization

BY

DR. JOSEFA IOTEYKO

*Formerly head of the Laboratory of Psycho-Physiology at
Brussels University, Laureate of the Institute
and of the Academy of Medicine
In charge of the course on "Fatigue" at the Collège de
France in 1916*

———

The human motor and the measurement of industrial fatigue—
Scientific management—Measurement of aptitudes—Anthropological comparison of the sexes from the point of view
of strength and endurance—Alimentation and work—
Re-education of the left hand for the mutilated—Belgian
methods of technical education and the University of Labour

———

LONDON:

GEORGE ROUTLEDGE & SONS, LIMITED

NEW YORK: E. P. DUTTON & CO.

———

1919

PREFACE

IN this little volume we have collected together a series of
articles published in 1916 and 1917 in the *Revue
Philosophique,* the *Revue Scientifique,* and the *Revue
Générale des Sciences.* We have revised them to ensure
that continuity of thought which has always run through
them all, but which does not shew quite so distinctly in
scattered publications ; to these we have added the
substance of some of our lectures on *Fatigue* delivered at
the *Collège de France.*

The leading idea running through this collection has
been the necessity for throwing light on certain points
in industrial psycho-physiology, which is universally
recognised as important at the decisive hour through
which we are now passing. Close collaboration between
science and industry will be necessary in the near future ;
the importance of this alliance will be greater than ever
when the actual crisis is passed and the need for making
a fresh start and for increased activity has made itself
felt. Now, events have caused a scarcity of labour ;
it is, therefore, necessary to partly supply its place by
as perfect and scientific an organisation of labour as is
possible. A great part of life will have to be re-constructed.
It is important that this reconstruction should be well
devised from the first start, and that it should be based
upon scientific rules, so that the unhappy errors of the
past may be avoided.

This necessity has been so clearly seen that the attention of the Paris Academy of the Sciences has recently
been drawn to the importance of the problem, and various
measures have been proposed.

In the present volume we shall examine certain aspects
of the question, and add some personal contributions

collected in the course of investigations of many years' duration on the problem of Fatigue in the motor function.

Four problems are examined :—

The first concerns the *Human Motor*, and here the question of apprenticeship, the manner of the economic working of the body, and the limits of industrial fatigue form the chief part.

The second is devoted to *Taylor's System*, which is so much discussed at the present time.

The third relates to the relative *Aptitude for Work of the Right Hand and of the Left Hand*, a question the importance of which has become very real, on account of the large numbers of men maimed in the war. We shall examine in succession : the estimate of the strength, and of the power of endurance of each hand, in the case of man and of woman, comparatively ; we shall advance a new theory of our own regarding right-handedness ; we shall give some rules for the re-education of the motor power of the wounded, and closely examine the process of writing with the left hand.

Finally, the fourth problem deals with the *Belgian Methods of Technical Education*. We have thought that it would not be uninteresting to make these known, since Belgium now occupies the foremost place in productivity in proportion to her population. She owes this productivity to her methods of industrial and technical education.

We trust that the importance of the problems discussed justify the publication of this volume and that it will emphasize the interest already felt in the subject.

TABLE OF CONTENTS

CONTENTS

CONTENTS

CONTENTS

The Science of Labour.

I.

THE HUMAN MOTOR.

I.—DEFINITION OF THE PROBLEM.

Amongst the numerous researches relating to
man, undertaken by modern science, those which
are connected with his physical fitness for work
are certainly amongst the most important. The
human being, in these investigations, is looked upon
as a motor to which chemical energy is supplied,
which is restored to the world in the form of
mechanical labour and heat.

All animals may be compared to motors, which
transform the energy with which they have been
supplied. But they differ from inanimate motors in
that the cycle of transformations is not reversible
in the case of the living motor, and the energy which

is given it must invariably be of a chemical nature. Moreover, the living motor can act only intermittently ; fatigue and the need of sleep overtake it, and forcibly interrupt the course of its activity.

The human motor may be studied from two very different points of view. On the one hand, it is a question of *laboratory researches*, having for their chief object the verification of the laws governing the transformation of energy in the living being. Studies of this nature have been carried on in every country, but principally by Chauveau in Paris, Atwater and Benedict in the United States, Rübner, Züntz, and Loewy in Germany. We must also remember the " Laboratoire d'Energétique" founded by Ernest Solvay near the Physiological Institute of the University of Brussels. This laboratory has been in existence only four years. Amongst successful work achieved there, we may mention the experiments made by ourselves in collaboration with M. Ch. Henry, on muscles ; on a law of diminution of effort shewn by the ergograph (*C. R., of the Academy of the Sciences*, 30 March, 1903) ; on the general equation of the curves of fatigue (*C.R.*, 24 August, 1903) ; on the modifications of the ergographic constants under various experimental conditions (*C.R.*, 24 May, 1904) ; on a connection between labour and the labour known as stationary, which, according to the ergograph, are energetically equivalent (*C.R.*, 28 December, 1903) ; on the limits and on the laws of the variations of available energy, according to the ergograph, following the frequency of the contractions, and the weight lifted. (*C.R.*, 28 November, 1904). By the use of the apparatus known by the name of the *Calorimetric Chamber*, Atwater was enabled to submit both the physical and the intellectual toil of man to a most rigorous test, from the standpoint of the transformations of energy.

On the other hand, we have to consider the application of the subject to *the study of industrial labour*, and this study can be pursued as well in the laboratories as in the factories and the workshops. The immediate object of these enquiries is very different from the former. It is not impossible, within the impassable limits of the law of the conservation of energy, to communicate an activity to the human motor which will favour the liberation of one form of energy rather than of another ; we are thinking of exterior, mechanical energy, the only kind which is of use in industrial work, and which should therefore rank above internal energy, which cannot be used. Following the principle of the conservation of energy, which has been indisputably verified on the muscles, the heat given off, and the me-

chanical work produced, will be found to be
equivalent ; that which the human motor gains
on the one hand, it loses on the other. Furthermore, stationary work is often sterile work, convert-
ing itself integrally into heat and resolving itself
into intense fatigue. The general principle for the
production of useful work is admitted ; there is
still room for the choice of the most appropriate
movements, those best adapted to attain the end
in view ; certain movements are exhausting and
unproductive, either because they are made too
slowly or with an effort out of proportion to the
result obtained, or because they are badly localized, since they put one articulation in motion
in place of another, etc.

Hence the idea of submitting the working
of the bodily organs to experimental tests with a
view to discover their best working conditions,
to detect fatigue, and to lay down a scientific
basis for industrial work. We may call the
results achieved by researches in this sphere the
" Science of Labour," for, although this study
is only in its infancy, it has the benefit of all
preceding researches of pure science which will
give it their authoritative support in its noble
desire that the working classes may benefit by the
physiological and psychological discoveries of
our century.   One of the promoters of this move-

ment was the lamented Hector Denis, Deputy to the Belgian Chamber, who with incomparable ardour never ceased to encourage his fellow-citizens in those researches of which he foresaw the interest and utility. .

II.—THE PROBLEM OF APPRENTICESHIP.

Industrial evolution gives an ever-increasing importance to the psychic factor in the artisan's work, says Omer Buyse[1], formerly director of the Université de Travail at Charleroi, now director of that at Brussels.

The phenomenon known as the "Crisis of Apprenticeship" is mainly due, according to this author, to the want of harmony between the old form of apprenticeship and the technical capacity requisite at the present day. Man, even now, very rarely works as a physical motor in the industries of ancient Europe. Man works more and more as a psycho-physiological apparatus. The problem of industrial labour, therefore, cannot be dealt with simply as a branch of mechanics applied to the natural sciences ; there is mixed with it a *psychic element* which we recognise by its manifestations, but of the causes of which we are still

Omer Buyse, *Le probleme psycho-physique de l'Apprentisage (Revue Psychologique*, Vol. iii, 1910, pp. 377-399, Brussels).

ignorant. The growing importance of the psychic factor will displace the axis of enquiry in the field of psycho-physiology. The manner of working, the dynamic effort, the duration of pauses, etc., introduce elements of variation in the expenditure of energy and the amount of useful work supplied, which depend on the psychic qualities of the individual from the standpoint of productiveness both as to quantity and quality (Buyse).

Omer Buyse did his utmost to discover the period of the psycho-physiological factors which come into play during apprenticeship in the wood and iron trades, by watching the work of four young workmen in different stages of proficiency for several months, and from day to day, and that of some student mechanical-fitters, electricians, modellers and joiners from the School of Handicrafts, as well. From these observations one dominating fact stands out ; through all the changes to which industry has been subjected *the value of the workmanship always is, and will for ever remain, the decisive element in the development of the capacity of production.* Engineers and inventors apply themselves ceaselessly to perfecting tools and the means of manufacture by working out ideas supplied by science, but these experimenters do not seem to have paid sufficient attention to the perfecting of the human motor.

The introduction of automatic and semi-automatic tools and of the system of serial operations profoundly modify the qualities required in a workman. Under what conditions should the work of a craftsman be accomplished so as to attain its best economic result ? It can be admitted as possible that this question may be answered by the investigations of experimental physiology in conjunction with mechanical measurements made upon rudimentary industrial labour. One may hope, Omer Buyse remarks with justice, that systematic study may soon lead us to an exact knowledge of the physiological and psychological qualities upon which the fitness of a craftsman rests. The orientation which some professors of technical education, in collaboration with some experimental physiologists, actually give to their researches enables us to foresee the not far distant time when they will remove, with their registering appliances, into the factories and workshops and into the timber-yards themselves, there to make scientific enquiries concerning the training and the work of the artisan. Examination of the economic problem of labour resolves itself into (*a*) the subject : the power, the apprentice, the workman ; and (*b*) the object : the resistance, the work to be accomplished in typical industries.

Omer Buyse goes on to say that the physical attitude of the workman as he works has a great influence on the amount of work he accomplishes. By discovering the voluntary degree of economy of energy that it is possible to effect in the handling of old-fashioned tools, in prescribing attitudes which lead to a minimum of expenditure of energy for a given piece of work, laboratory researches may have a considerable influence on the productivity of the worker.

Hence, says Buyse, the effect of training or habit (a state antagonistic to fatigue), is to augment the ease, the speed, the accuracy, and the uniformity of an act by its repetition. It may be referred to one thing ; the adaptation of the psycho-physical apparatus to certain ~particular conditions of action. By the repetition of a movement an aptitude is acquired for doing it without the conscious intervention of the will or the attention ; consequently, training effects an economy of nervous flux and relieves the strain on the central nervous system. In the second place, under the influence of training, the involuntary movements which, at the beginning, are made in co-operation with the principal movement, are suppressed. These involuntary movements are a characteristic sign of inaptitude, and constitute a waste of energy. Practice leads the body to put those muscles whose action is inconvenient out of play, and to employ only those which do the work with the greatest economy and the minimum of effort. The mechanical nature of work which results from training, attains its maximum in the movements of the small muscles whose expenditure of the flux of excitation in isolated contractions is manifestly less than that exacted by putting the large muscles in motion. The introduction of machinery in production has lightened the task of the large muscles at the expense of the small ones. *The principle of the small muscles is at the bottom of the evolution of labour.*

An important constituent element in industrial intelligence is *voluntary attention and concentration.* It is thus that, in the midst of the noises and bustle of a factory, the machinist remains turned towards the machine which is performing his work. The psycho-physical aptitudes which seem to be peculiarly favourable to industrial work would, according to Buyse, appear to be the rapidity and the precision of movement ; these characteristics are the expression of the degree of control that the worker possesses over his movements, and their coordination.

Another indication of aptitude appears in an

interesting phenomenon which accompanies the period of apprenticeship, it is the estimation of the amount of fatigue produced in overcoming resistance of the tool, in industrial work.

This estimate bears upon two different quantities : (1) the muscular effort connected with the execution of the work ; (2) the nervous effort due to the fact that the nervous centres, according to Ioteyko, transmit to the muscles an excitation, the strength of which is in direct proportion to the inertia of the muscle (Buyse).

Our investigations have in effect shewn that the intensity of [1] nervous effort increases as the mechanical conditions of the work required of the muscles become more difficult, and inversely that the intensity of the nervous effort diminishes when the muscular work to be done becomes more easy (law of the economy of effort).   In this we have a remarkable instance of the automatic regulation of nervous effort, the difficulties of the work acting as a stimulant to the nerve-centres.

Buyse investigates this question from the standpoint of apprenticeship.   This automatic regulation is acquired by experience, and depends upon

[1] J. Ioteyko, *Les Lois, de l'Ergograph : Etude physiologique et Mathematique.   Bull. de l'Académie de Belgique, classe des Sciences,* 1904, pp. 557-726 ; 2nd Ed. in the *Annales d'Electrobiologie,* 1905.   See also ; J. Ioteyko, *La loi de l'Economie de l'effort en dynamique nerveuse.*   Communicated to the Sixth International Physiology Congress of Brussels, 1904.

an estimate of the intensity of the effort required for the performance of the work, made probably by the perception of the fatigue which will result from the work. Apprenticeship which leads to a realization of economy in labour is the regulator of the muscular effort, which succeeds nervous action. Muscular and nervous attempts at action, like the succeeding judgments as to the effort put forth, are not haphazard and un-directed.

They are methodical, and the method consists in attacking the particular work to be done in the manner suggested by past experience. By this means, and by means of a series of mistakes, each recognized in turn, it becomes possible to adjust the neuro-muscular excitation more accurately to the action required. Apprentice-ship to industries is carried out on the experi-mental method. A beginner, who has no know-ledge whatever regarding the effort required for cutting wood is prepared to make a considerable effort in order to perform the work successfully ; he tires, and thus gets some idea, some estimate of the effort to be made. To make hypotheses, says Buyse, to put them to the best of experience, to rectify them until you come to some provi-sional or definite conclusion, to eliminate from the error another of less importance, until you get near the truth, is to simply apply the experimental method, the method of discovery.

III.—ECONOMIC METHOD OF WORKING THE BODY.

The investigations of Mosso, and of his collaborators at the University of Turin, have opened the road to these researches. They are too well known to need repetition here. An exhaustive study has been made by Italian physiologists of the various conditions governing the optimum of work with regard to the weight to be lifted, the speed of contraction, intervals for rest, etc.

After writing our theories for the Doctorate of Medicine, prepared in Paris, in M. Ch. Richet's laboratory, we devoted more than fifteen years to the study of physical and intellectual fatigue in the Physiological Institute, Brussels, and in other laboratories.[1]

We owe to M. Imbert, Professor in the Faculty of Medicine at Montpellier, a very attractive

See some of our publications : *Fatigue* (article in the *Dictionnaire de Physiologie*, of Ch. Richet, nearly 200 pp., 1903); *La Fonction Musculaire* (Doin, Paris, 1909) ; *Le quotient de la Fatigue* (*C.R. de l'Académie des Sciences*, 1900) ; *Effets du travail de certains groupes musculaires sur d'autres groupes qui ne font aucun travail* (*Ibid.*, 1900) ; *Participation des centres nerveux aux phénomènes de fatigue musculaire* (*Année Psychol*, VII, 1900) ; *Le travail des centres nerveux spinaux* (*C.R.*, 1900) ; *Les lois de l'Ergographie : étude physiologique et Mathématique* (*Travaux de l'Institut Solvay de Physiologie.* Pamphlet of 172 pp., 1904).

study on the economic method of working the body.[2]

We cannot, by the exercise of our will, modify the form of our muscles ; but it is not without interest to know whether our various muscles, in so far as they are motors, are sufficiently defective in their natural form to entail a useless expenditure of energy, or whether they are not so. By reason of the mechanical conditions under which the levers of the body operate, the intensity of the force of muscular contraction varies during the moving of a load, or even during the stationary holding of a weight, according to the position of the bone-lever used. Now, it generally depends upon our will as to whether we adopt this or that position for our bone-lever, in order to accomplish some exterior and pre-determined task, and we thus do exercise some volitional influence upon our total expenditure of energy. Imbert says, that it is a fascinating idea to think that our body, so far as it is only a productive instrument of toil, is constructed upon a general plan and presents such harmony of action that all useless expenditure of energy is, or at least may be, avoided. This point of view is inexact. And even fatigue, which seems to be the most important criterion

[2] A. Imbert, *Mode de fonctionnement économique de l'organisme* (*Collection Scientia*), 1902.

of expenditure of energy, may correspond to different expenditures of energy, if we compare different motors, bodies which are not in identically the same state of action. Moreover, the idea of mechanical work, which is independent of the time employed in performing it, is purely abstract.

If it is by fatigue that we wish to judge of the total expenditure of energy, the limits between which this expenditure may vary should be attentively studied, so that the reaction of the organism to sufficiently marked variations of sensation may be clearly noted. Imbert was anxious that children should not be included in these experiments. For them, physical exercise, the expenditure of mechanical energy, is a physiological necessity, almost as necessary as food ; they spend from the need of spending ; they run and jump instead of keeping to the economic gait of walking ; they even prefer a painful ascent by a rope to the less exhausting process of going up a staircase. The natural and unconscious pre-occupation of children is not, as it is with the grown man, to discover how to make the best use of power, but, by exercise, to encourage the normal development of the human motor. In short, they are not perfect motors, but motors in course of formation. Now, in contrast with children, from the standpoint of the utilization of their strength, are convalescents. They seek for the strictest economy of force ; they do all they can to lessen such work as involves vertical displacement of the centre of gravity.

Imbert cites an interesting incident investigated by Haughton, relating to a road traversed by some English fisherwomen. The work of these women was the gathering of shellfish, and they had to go along a road between their village and the shore. The ground to be crossed consisted of two very different stretches, so far as ease of walking was concerned—one was firm and resisted the pressure of the feet, the other was sandy, the absence of firmness necessitating a greater expenditure of energy for the same rate of walking. On account of this peculiarity, the road which entailed the lesser expenditure of energy was not, geometrically, the shorter way, that is to say, the straight line, because the straight line would have compelled a long walk over the sandy piece of ground. Neither of these paths was that followed by the fisher-women. The path chosen was midway between the two and it was just this one that corresponded to the minimum expenditure of energy. Haughton decided mathematically that the law followed in this walk was analogous to the law of refraction, by following which, light waves passing through media having different densities, are transmitted from point to point in a minimum of time and with a minimum of effort. In other words, by choosing the intermediate road, partly composed of firm soil and partly of sand, the fisherwomen were able to accomplish the journey in the minimum of time, and with the minimum production of fatigue.

Other examples, in various spheres, could be cited, all demonstrating the constant tendency of the human organism to reduce its expenditure of energy to a minimum. The movements of the eye form a good example of a natural adaptation for effecting this object, the eye, on leaving one object and fixing another, revolving about an axis perpendicular to a plane cutting both the former and the new line of vision. This is known as Listing's law, and shews that the eye normally makes the smallest possible movement in transferring its line of vision from one object to another.

Generally, it is by a forward inclination of the body that we diminish the amplitude of the vertical movements of our centre of gravity. We also assume this stooping attitude when walking quickly, or from fatigue, or, again, when we are over-weighted by too heavy a load, that is to say, under the various circumstances for which it becomes necessary to expend the maximum effort. Imbert draws attention to the *antagonistic* muscles. There are very few muscles that are really antagonistic (as are, for example, the internal and external rectus muscles of the eye). Other muscles are either in direct accord, or else, without ceasing to be antagonistic, can co-operate simultaneously for the achievement of a common purpose, as Demeny has observed. For instance, we see, in slow movements of uniform speed, that there is a simultaneous contraction of the two antagonistic muscles. Now a force constantly and always acting in the same manner on a body will give it a quickened motion ; it follows, therefore, that sustained speed can be obtained only if the action of the flexing or extending muscle is each moment counterbalanced by an inverse action of the antagonistic muscle whose intervention is indispensable. It is different directly the movements executed became rapid. The mechanical reason for the intervention of the antagonistic muscle then no longer exists ; also it appears that this muscle remains relaxed, except at the end of a movement, when it intervenes to cancel the speed. In all these cases expenditure is reduced and the work increased.

B

It is just the same with the form of the muscles, which, according to Haughton's observations, is strictly adapted to the nature of the work to be done, such as the heart for example, where the complex arrangement of the muscular fibres renders them particularly suitable for utilization to the performance of the work required of that organ. W. Roux has likewise demonstrated the perfect harmony existing between the form of the muscles and the conditions of their work. The variations in the length of the fibres are adapted to the extent of the movements which the muscles have to make, and we see the muscular fibres extend themselves spontaneously when stretching to a part of their length, and vice versa. Marsy definitely solved this problem in the affirmative.

Finally, Imbert cites the work done by de Chauveau, to whom was reserved the discovery of the first laws of muscular energy. His investigations having become classic, we will not recapitulate them here, but we must remember that they dealt chiefly with the evolution of the internal work of the muscles by virtue of the principle of Equivalence, which governs all transformations of energy. His experiments were carried out upon the flexors of the fore-arm in man, whose conditions of work vary according to circumstances.

The outcome of all these experiments is, says Imbert, that, in the mechanical movements as well as in the conservation of the internal energy of the muscles, one clearly sees the unconscious but constant effort to reduce the total expenditure of energy to a minimum and the voluntary realisation of mechanical conditions corresponding to this minimum of expenditure. The body thus would appear to be apt to appreciate two kinds of conditions, the first external and of a mechanical nature, the second internal and of a physiological nature ; it would seem to know how to keep account at the same time of mathematical laws and of biological laws, but it is always by the same process that it arrives at conclusions which differ in their essence. The working of the animated motor is, in effect, influenced by that very working itself ; all work, sufficient in duration and quantity, entails fatigue, and it is in reality by the constant effort to avoid fatigue that we regulate our action (Imbert).

The protective part played by fatigue, which we dealt with in a previous publication,[1] is fully confirmed by these investigations.

We have previously seen that, according to Buyse, at the time of apprenticeship, that is to

[1] J. Ioteyko, *Les Défenses psychiques : I. La Douleur ; II. La Fatigue. Revue Philosophique*, Feb. 1913.

say, during the psychic adaptation to the work, we became conscious of the nervous effort required for over-coming the external resistance offered to our performance of the work. At first the movements are accomplished at the expense of a great waste of energy, but repeated attempts lead to economy in movements. The decisive movement here is the consciousness of the effort required. In the investigations connected with the method of the economic working of the body (outside the phase of apprenticeship), this decisive movement which regulates the conservation of its energy is the feeling of fatigue. Now, effort and fatigue are correlated sensations, for a great effort invariably leads to fatigue, and when a young apprentice, in the course of time, acquires the best movements, it is because he is convinced by experience that they lead to the minimum of fatigue.

We are, therefore, justified in affirming that the psychic factor which regulates the expenditure of energy of the human motor, so as to ensure the most economical working, the factor which guides the animal machine to adaptation to the best conditions for working, which even modifies the forms of muscles to suit them to their work, is the sensation of fatigue. We know that the function creates the organ. The importance of fatigue from the standpoint of evolution is here transparently clear.

The wrong movements, badly adapted, accompanied by a waste of energy, are those that, at the same time, are the most fatiguing ; now, pain and fatigue are the physical and psychical conditions which we are endeavouring to avoid throughout our lives. Fatigue is the consciousness of over-work, the result, it may be, of too much work, or it may be unproductive work, accompanied by waste.

Is fatigue supreme ? It certainly is not more so than all our other psychic defences, such as, for example, pain, whose defensive role has been so thoroughly investigated by Charles Richet. Even the general law of pain and of pleasure may, in certain cases, be opposed to happiness. The part played by fatigue could be exercised only within certain limits. Like all sensations, fatigue is subject to illusions, to oscillations, it may become insensible in some pathological conditions, or, on the contrary, be unduly developed without apparent cause. It is, moreover, subject to the conditions of work. It is easy to understand that the aberrations are more frequent when the work is very complicated as, for example, in the case of industrial work. Le Chatelier is, therefore, right when he protests against the supposition that skilled workmen understand quite well how to make the best use of their forces in order to obtain a given result with the minimum amount of fatigue.

If we take, as an example, the transport of heavy weights, a task which is relatively simple, we find, according to Taylor, that the labour is governed by six variables, viz., the weight carried on each journey, the distance traversed, the inclination of the road, the speed when fully loaded, the speed of the return empty-handed, and the time of rest. The workman could not in any case determine under these conditions the most economical use of his mechanical energy.

In other cases a dozen or more variables have been counted. Taylor devoted 25 years of his life to making exact calculations concerning these variables, and their large number prevents the workman himself from taking any bearings. We may conclude that the sense of fatigue ceases to be really protective under these conditions, which moreover nature could not have foreseen. This sense partly loses its biological significance here, not because there is anything out of harmony with natural laws, but because the body is not adapted to all these new functions imposed upon it by modern industries. Consequently, it is no longer the sense of fatigue which can be the decisive *moment* to which is allotted the task of regulating the *optimum* of work. When dealing with industrial labour this task is handed over to another factor. We are contemplating scientific *investigations* of the conditions of the work itself, the measurement of, not only subjective, but also objective, fatigue.

4.—THE MEASURE OF INDUSTRIAL FATIGUE.

The problem of labour could never have been solved had it not been for the entry of physiology and psychology into its domain.[1]

Therefore, relying upon facts authenticated by Mosso, and upon other considerations we find that fatigue increases much more rapidly as the duration of the work done is prolonged.[2]

Mosso [1] has shewn, by means of the ergograph, that the exhaustion of our bodies does not increase in direct ratio with the work accomplished, therefore, the performance of work two or three times more arduous does not produce fatigue two or three times as great. The important fact to remember is, however, that a given task per-

[1] J. Ioteyko, La Mesure de la Fatigue professionnelle. Revue psychologique II, 1909, p. 53 Bruxelles.

[2] J. Ioteyko, *Les Defenses Psychiques. Revue philosophique*, Feb. 1913. This article contains other details bearing on the question.

[1] A. Mosso, *La fatigue intellectuelle et physique*, Paris, F. Alcan 1894.

formed by an already fatigued muscle has a much more injurious effect upon that muscle, and results in the production of greater fatigue than would be the case if the same task were performed under normal conditions.

The human organism cannot be compared to a locomotive which consumes a given quantity of coal for each mile of road it covers ; when the body is tired a small amount of labour produces disastrous effects. In these experiments the accumulation of fatigue was measured by means of the time necessary for complete restoration to the normal.

We studied [2] the accumulation of fatigue by means of short rests between the ergographic curves. The same rest produced a diminishing effect in proportion as the muscle became more and more fatigued. Identical phenomena were observable in the domain of intellectual fatigue.

This proof, we maintain, shews the necessity of raising wages, not in proportion to the increase of labour, not uniformly for each additional hour of work, but on a graduated scale, seeing that the wear and tear of the body proceeds in geometrical progression, whilst the work is accomplished in arithmetical progression. It also proves that human energy is opposed to over-work, the work

[2] J. Ioteyko, *Les lois de l'Ergographic*, quoted above.

itself becoming less and less productive in proportion to the growth of fatigue. The reduction of the hours of work thus become a biological and economic necessity.[1]

Hence we can formulate the following postulates which social science should take into consideration, seeing that they are derived from statements scientifically and experimentally proved.

1. That as the daily work of the workman follows an arithmetical progression, so his wages should follow a geometrical progression. The co-efficient in the increase of salaries should be experimentally determined in each trade by taking into consideration the methods of work employed.

2. For equal work, an equal wage. The woman who does the same work as the man should be paid the same wage. The amount of work done should be determined in each trade. An equivalence might be established between the various trades based on the laws of energy. This postulate, which is that of justice, based on the equality of production, nowhere comes into collision with that of justice based on an equality of expense. It is thus, for example, that, by

[1] See : L. J. Fromont, *Une expérience industrielle de la journée de travail.* Published by l'Institut Solvay de Sociologie, 1906. Brussels.

reason of a different principle, fathers of
large families have a right to supplementary
grants.

3. It is necessary to put a maximum limit
to the daily number of working hours for
each trade. On account of the inevitable
wear and tear of the body, an excessive
increase in the number of working hours
cannot be compensated for, by an increase
of wages.

4. In the educational world teachers expose
themselves to grave disappointment when
they increase the amount of the pupils' work
without knowing the laws of fatigue in
relation to their age, sex, constitution, and
aptitudes. The difficulty to be surmounted
does not increase in proportion to the matter
to be studied, but much more rapidly
(Ebbringhaus).

Those subjects which demand a high degree of
training by means of prolonged periods of study
cannot be acquired by an organism in a state of
over-work. To solve the question scientifically
it is necessary to demonstrate that the worker is
over-worked, that is to say, that his physiological
expenditure is in excess of his receipts. In order
to avoid over-work it is necessary that the worker

should recover his full powers by his night's rest and his weekly rest.

How are these results to be estimated ? The matter is all the more difficult in that, to over-work, are often added the injurious effects of an unhealthy trade. There is, therefore, a double danger. It would be interesting to study this combination of two morbid effects, but it would also appear to be indispensable that the effects of fatigue should stand out in all their clearness if investigations are to be conducted in a strictly scientific fashion, so as to yield useful data.

It is absurd, says Liesse,[1] to pretend to fix *a priori* a uniform length of working-day for all industries in all countries.

The analysis of the elements of production teach us, on the contrary, that there exist different limits for each kind of work, often for each country investigated, the nature of the climate, the race and the habits of the people being the primary causes of the diversity. Sommerfeld [1] shares this opinion.

What methods can be advocated for studies of this kind ? The pathological method has far too long been the only one applied ; that consists

---

[1] A. Liesse, *Le travail au point de vere scientifique, industriel et social, Paris,* F. Alcan, 1899.

[1] Th. Sommerfeld, *Traité des maladies professionnelles.* French translation, Brussels, 1901.

in drawing up statistics of morbidity and mortality. Such a method, by itself, is insufficient, seeing that the pathogenetic action of fatigue is the sign of such serious trouble that it would be dangerous to base labour legislation on an organic collapse due to over-work. The methods advocated should be more delicate and at the same time more precise, allowing of the measuring, so to speak, of the phenomena of fatigue and their manifestations, so as to put in evidence the signs of over-work long before organic collapse. It is a question of actual *prophylaxy of fatigue.* Such methods can be only psycho-physiological.

Fatigue is a very complex result of numerous factors. The intensity of the fatigue is the function of the following factors [1] :—

1. Hours of work.
2. Relative wages (ratio between a living wage and the cost of provisions).
3. Nature and organisation of the work.
4. Individual constitution and aptitudes (stature, length of arm, disposition of the muscles, power of attention, morbid predispositions, maladies).
5. Age.
6. Sex.
7. Town or country life.

[1] See our article in the *Revue Physiologique,* 1909.

8. Personal hygiene (nourishment, sleep, etc. A workman may spend his wages on useless, or even harmful things. Moral Hygiene).

One may add to these factors the influence of climate, of race, of customs, etc. Amongst these factors the nature and organisation of the work comprise many chapters, and it is chiefly here that research should be made ; but no formal conclusion can be arrived at without consulting the conditions collectively under which the work is carried on. These conditions are to the worker *intrinsic* and *extrinsic*.

The question of industrial fatigue was placed on the programme for discussion at the International Congress of Hygiene and Demography. The Congress, held at Brussels in 1903, put the question in the following form : *To what extent is it possible by physiological methods, to study fatigue, its manifestations, and its degrees in the various industries ? What are the arguments which the physiological and medical science could or might recommend in favour of definite methods for the organisation of labour ?* Three reports and one paper were submitted in reply to this question (Imbert, Treves, Demoor, and ourselves). Seeing that the problem was so new, not one of these writers was able to give the result of experiments, but they all at least made an attempt to solve it.

In our article we suggested a plan of study which included the following points :

I. *Preliminary Medical Examination.*—The first obvious necessity is the medical examination of young people at the time when they are choosing a career, and this applies just as much to the various handicrafts as it does to the liberal professions. All those who have taken the wrong turning in their choice of a career become an easy prey to over-work and only aggravate existing defects. Their efficiency is seriously diminished, and consequently their well-being. In these inaptitudes in certain professions, we may detect one of the causes of over-work, and social unproductiveness.

II. *Laboratory methods which have for their aim* the study of the energy of labour.

III. *Investigations and experiments made on the workers, in factories, workshops, and buildings.*
   1. *The study of fatigue in different parts of the body* (organs of the senses, etc.).
   2. *Observations made on the progress of the work done.* It is essential to see which conditions yield the best return.

3. *Influence of machinery on the over-fatigue of the workers.*

4. *Sensitivity to pain.* Sensitivity to pain, measured by the algesimeter, increases under the influence of slight intellectual fatigue, and diminishes under great exhaustion Itoyko and Stefanowska).

5. *Ergographic methods.*[1]

6. *The ponometric method.* The ponometer is the instrument invented by Mosso to inscribe the curve of nervous effort during the progress of muscular work.

7. *Method of the reflex phenomena.*—In the case of cerebral fatigue, as the inhibitory effects of the brain on the central nervous system become less, the reflexes becomes exaggerated. This fact has been observed in neurasthenia and also in cases of general fatigue (Westpole, Sternberg).

8. *Method of chromatic sensitivity.* This sensitivity becomes less in cases of general fatigue.

9. *Plethysmographic method.*—Under fatigue it is noticeable that the capillary pulse indicates *asthenia* (Binet and Courtier).

10. *Method of measuring the time taken for reaction.*—Reaction is slower under the influence of fatigue.

[1] See our book : *La fonction Musculaire* (Paris).

IV. *Pathological Methods.*—These consist in studying pathogenic effects of over-work ; loss of weight, arrested growth, deviations, malformations, industrial maladies.

V. *Investigations and interrogations.*—We would call attention to the interesting investigations made by Bloch (of Paris) on the subject of industrial fatigue. The author propounded the following question to different artisans ; When you have been very busy, whereabouts do you feel fatigue ? The answers, at first sight, seem very paradoxical ; we select a few examples. The baker, who had been kneading all night, leaning over and mixing the heavy mass of dough, complained of fatigue in his legs. The blacksmith, who strikes the anvil, does not complain of tired arms or shoulders, but of his back and loins. The road-mender working with his pick is tired in the legs. The shoemaker, who strikes with a hammer, complains of his loins and abdominal muscles. The young soldier, after a march, is chiefly tired in the nape of the neck, even though he has not carried a haversack. The inexperienced violinist complains of a distressing strain at the back of the neck ; whilst the accomplished artist wails over a numbness of the left hand which he has held contracted upon the fingerboard of his instrument. The experienced oarsman suffers from fatigue in the calves of his legs and insteps, after prolonged exertion.

The paradoxical appearance of the answers is explained in the following way by Bloch : the fatigue predominates in the groups of muscles that become immovable when contracted. These experiments shew the existence of *static* fatigue, which sometimes predominates. They also shew that the groups of auxiliary muscles in industrial movements should be exercised as much as possible so as to break the continuity of contractions, whether auxiliary or principal.

In his report laid before the Brussels Congress Imbert particularly insists upon the slackening of contraction and muscular relaxation which is the first sign of fatigue and manifests itself after quite a small number of contractions, even before the height of the movement is appreciably diminished. The fact, long known and noticed in the muscles of the frog, has been verified by Imbert and Gagniere in a man working at the ergograph. This diminution of the rapidity of contraction gives rise to a practical result of great interest.

The accidents in connection with labour are generally the outcome of some fortuitous event. In such cases they often arise so suddenly that the workman finds it is impossible to escape from the

C

danger that threatens. In other cases, on the contrary, the menace is less sudden ; the workman sees it coming, and can ward it off. But then it is necessary that the workman's muscular contraction should be achieved as rapidly as possible, because the time at the workman's disposal is often only a fraction of a second. And in those trades where the workmen are, as it were, attached to a moving machine and have to regulate the speed of their work by that of the machine it is easy to conceive the part played by fatigue in workmen's accidents. Besides, one has also to take mental fatigue into consideration, and it is this which lengthens the psychic process intervening between perception and movement.

The result of this, says Imbert, is that accidents connected with work must be more numerous as the day advances, more numerous, too, in the corresponding hours, at the end than at the beginning of the week, if work is pressed too far. The statistics of the distribution of accidents connected with labour therefore constitute an indication of the degree of fatigue in the human motor (see later).

Other observations may also lead to the verification of physical fatigue. The attitude of the workman at the beginning and at the end of a hard day's work may shew certain modifications, which follow the principle discovered by Marey, in connection with the vertical displacements of the centre of gravity during progress of the work. As a general rule, the useless expenditure of energy is suppressed during fatigue and the body instinctively adopts a more economical attitude. This attitude can be determined by chronophotography which also enables successive records to be taken during the progress of work.[1] Whether the question is one of intellectual, or of physical, fatigue, can now be decided, as we have since then been in possession of general methods of investigation, and of general processes of measurement. Such is the conclusion arrived at in Imbert's report [2]

In an article which appeared in *L'Année Psychologique* Imbert shews the importance of the problem laid down by social medicine. However useful these attempts may be, we must not ignore the almost hostile indifference with which they were at first received in the Syndicalist centres of working men. Moreover, the experimental

[1] In an exhaustive inquiry into the labour of working men undertaken by the Solvay Institute of Sociology in Brussels, in which we, in colloboration with others, undertook the physiological part, the attitudes of workmen were determined, thanks to cinematography. Events and the tragic accident of which M. Waxwieiler, director of the Institute, was the victim, delayed the publication of the inquiry.

[2] Imbert, *L'Etude scientifique expérimentale du travail professionel* (*Année Psychologique*, 1907, Vol. xiii., pp. 245-259).

and exact study of a trade is a project which
cannot be carried out without some difficulty.
The author quite rightly insists on the inadequate
information furnished by the valuation of mechanical work ; as a matter of fact, this puts us in
possession of only one factor in the problem.
He gives an account of experiments he made on
the dock labourers at Cette in the unloading of
colliers as well as those of A. Gauthier on the labour
of wine and spirit storehouse workmen working
a wine-pump. In both cases the mechanical
labour was stringently estimated. But it would
be misleading to rely upon a simple estimate in
kilogramme-metres to fix the value of industrial
labour.

To compare in kilogrammes, labour achieved
under different conditions, would lead to the
conclusion, for instance, that to ascend to the
next floor by going up a good staircase is the
same thing as raising oneself by one's arms up a
long vertical rope, since the mechanical labour
is the same in both cases. Such a conclusion
is mechanically exact, but physiologically false.

Thus, the wine and spirit storehouse labourers,
studied by A. Gauthier accomplished, in their from
nine to ten hours' day, work estimated at 212,200
kilogramme-metres ; whilst the day's work of the
dock-labourers was equal to 75,000 kilogramme-

metres. Judging by these numerical results,
it would seem that the former labour must be
about three times as difficult as the latter, because
in these cases the same muscles came into play,
viz., those of the arms and of the trunk.   But the
mechanical conditions in which the muscles
operated in these two kinds of work are sufficiently
dissimilar to completely reverse the conclusion.
All the dock-labourers would be capable of performing the day's work of a wine pumper, but
the reverse would certainly not be the case.
Consequently the eight hours' day of the coalheaver
is paid at the rate of eight francs, whilst in the
same town the wage of the wine pumper is only
from 4-5 francs for a ten hours' day.

Compare with these figures the enormous
amount of mechanical work a postman would
produce who made two rounds daily, each of
three hours duration, at a speed of 3,600 metres
per hour.   We should thus get 259,200 kilogramme-
metres per day, whilst a dock labourer only
achieved 75,000 kilogramme-metres.

It is enough also to remember the works of
Chauveau dealing with internal muscular effort
(excess of animal heat), to judge of the well-
known inadequacy of an estimate based exclusively upon the information derived solely from
mechanical labour.

To estimate in kilogramme-metres is of practical use when the aim is to measure the relative values of different movements employed in the same work, etc. But if it is desired to study the effects that skilled labour may produce on the body of the labourer, research should be directed to the study of biological phenomena.

With regard to the literature on over-work submitted to the *XIVth International Congress on Hygiene and Demography*, held at Berlin in 1907, we here give an outline, based on the account given by Imbert.[1] Of the four reports submitted to the Congress upon the question of *Over-work in the performance of industrial labour*, those by Dr. Roth, by Dr. Treves, and by Professor Imbert assert the existence of overwork ; the third report, presented by Eisner, chief engineer to the Berlin Water Works, states the opposite view. Eisner's report—a very sincere one—is the expression of very strong and convinced opinions, and furnishes a partial explanation of the bitterness of the conflict between Capital and Labour.

The three other writers, a German, an Italian, and a Frenchman, all members of the Medical profession, testify in a greater or less degree, to the existence of over-work, not as a general

[1] Imbert, *Le surmenage par suite du travail professionnel au XIV Congrés international d'hygiene et de démographie*, Berlin 1907 (*Année Psychologique*, XIV, Vol. 1908).

fact affecting the working population as a whole
of the various countries, but particularly with
regard to certain districts or to certain categories
of workers. Treves, of Turin, expresses himself
as follows, " The work in the experimental
physiological and psychological laboratories would
be sterile and of very limited interest, if the doctor
in the course of his researches did not ask himself
which are, in practical life, the circumstances
equivalent to those created by his experiments.
We may say that, from whatever branch of
human knowledge it may emanate, every conception carried into the field of applied knowledge
implies some contribution to the solution of some
social problem, and we cannot eliminate the
social problem of labour when speaking of the
ætiology of industrial over-work."

The statistics of the accidents connected with
labour, which shed such a vivid light on the
phenomena of the fatigue of workmen, have
been studied by Imbert and Mestre.[1] In fact,
work engenders fatigue, and that is chiefly
produced by modifications which supervene
in the manner in which the motor at work acts,
and which consists in a slackening and diminution

[1] See : Imbert, *Les accidents de travail et les compagnies
d'Assurances (Revue scientifique,* 4 Juin, 1904). Imbert and
Mestre, *Statistiques d'accidents du travail.* Ibid., 24 Septembre,
1904).

in the intensity of the muscular contraction. The workman is all the less fit to perform the necessary defensive movements when an accident occurs, and to perform them with the required rapidity, in that he is admittedly weary.

It follows that the number of accidents should be greater when the workers are more tired, and the distribution of these accidents according to the time of day at which they occur should furnish a means of estimating the degree of fatigue felt by the workers who have been the victims of it.

Starting from this premise, the authors constructed a curve based on official information gathered from one district in Hérault, which numbers 56,458 workmen of various trades, subject to the law of accidents of labour, amongst whom there had been 2,065 acknowledged victims in 1903. In the next place, another curve was prepared, and that included, distributed according to the hours at which they occurred, the 660 accidents which had taken place in the industries officially known as *Management and Transport* (*Manutention et Transport*) which employ 6,695 workers. The results may be grouped as follows :
(1) The number of accidents increases progressively, from hour to hour during the first half-day ;
(2) After the fairly long mid-day rest, in the early hours of the second half-day, the number of

accidents is notably less than during the last
hour of the morning ; (3) In the course of the
second half of the day accidents again become
progressively more frequent from hour to hour ;
(4) The number of accidents per hour towards
the end of the second half-day is notably
higher than the corresponding maximum of the
morning.

We could not wish for stronger confirmation
of the Author's point of view, and the degree of
certainty is still further increased when we compare the two curves with one another and with the
curves of each trade which shew an identical
progression. Curves of this nature are nothing
new ; they are exactly like those that are obtained, for instance, when measuring intellectual
fatigue by means of the esthesiometric method.
And this is one more argument to oppose to those
who try to see in Imbert and Mestre's curves the
influence of chance or unknown cause other than
fatigue.

The authors also produce the results of other
statistics which, without exception, confirm
the same facts.

In basing arguments upon the number of
accidents, it is permissible to estimate the average
danger incurred in a given trade. The most
dangerous trades are those comprised under the

heading : *Chemical Industries ;* next comes *Management and Transport.*

We owe some other experimental writings on the measurement of industrial fatigue to Imbert., in collaboration with Mestre,[1] inspector of labour in Hérault, who has instituted researches relating to the transport of loads by means of a truck, a wheelbarrow with two low wheels in common industrial use.

One of the handles of this truck is made in two pieces, the portion grasped by the workman being joined to the other portion by means of two plates, one on either side of the handle, the attachment of the plates to the portion grasped by the workman being made with a single bolt so as to allow this portion to have a partial rotary movement in the vertical plane of the handle. On the under sides of the two portions of the handle are fixed two angle plates, interposed between, and fixed to which is an elliptical spring, whilst on the top sides of the two portions are fixed a second pair of similar angle plates, to one of which a Marey's tambour is attached, whilst to the other a rod is fixed which operates the diaphragm of the tambour by means of a link connection. By connecting the tambour to a receiving tambour

[1] Imbert and Mestre, *Recherches sur la manœuvre du Cabrouet et la fatigue qui en résulte.* Bulletin de l'inspection du travail, 1905, No. 5.

operating a stylus arranged to inscribe a record
on a drum, it is obvious that the efforts made
by the workman in a direction perpendicular
to the handles (that is the effort necessary to
support the load), can be registered. If the
other handle of the truck is made cylindrical
and the portion grasped by the workman is
surrounded by a sleeve, the lower end of which
is attached to a pair of angle irons similar to those
employed on the other handle, and located on the
upper and under sides of it, the same arrangement
of elliptical spring, tambour and rod being used
as before, the efforts of the workman in the
operation of pushing or pulling the truck can be
registered. In addition to the methods just
described, which were used to obtain a record of
the energy expended in supporting and transport-
ing loads by means of the truck (railway platform
truck), the energy required to load and unload the
truck was also registered by a modification of
the same device. This modification consisted
of an elliptical spring, atached to a hook and
provided with a handle, one side of the spring
carrying the transmitting tambour and the other
side the rod for operating the tambour diaphragm.
The workman grasped this device by the handle
and seized the load by means of the hook, his
effort in lifting or dragging the load on to or off

the truck was thus recorded on a revolving drum. Finally, one of Marey's boots was used to enable a record to be taken of the effort made by the workman on the axle of the truck wheels to check the recoil during loading of the truck.

All the efforts put forth by the workman during his work, both as to duration and intensity, could thus be registered. Of the various movements necessitated by the loading, transport, and the unloading, the most painful and the most tiring, because of its repetition, is that of loading. In order to place in the barrow a sack weighing 60 kilogrammes, the workman has to exert an effort of about 30 kilogrammes. Hence, a youth of about 16 or 17 years of age (these investigations especially have the labour of young workmen in view), can scarcely ever, under the mechanical conditions under which the load is handled, develop more than a maximum effort of 40 kilogrammes, it is, therefore, an effort equal to three quarters of the maximum which the young workman has to put out at each movement of loading. This movement being repeated sixty times an hour, for the transport of one sack to a distance of 48 metres, the young workman has thus, during the legal working day of ten hours, to put out with his upper limbs a total effort of more than 18,000 kilogrammes.

As to the actual transport, it is not very tiring on a firm soil, for a strength of from 3-4 kilogrammes suffices for the wheeling of a barrow loaded with a sack weighing 60 kilogrammes. On the other hand, one must seriously consider the total distance covered, which at the time these observations were made amounted to about 30 kilometres for the ten hours' work.

Finally, if, after having made a young workman labour for an hour, you give him two hours complete rest, the ergographic tracings then taken will still betray sufficiently marked signs of weariness.

The stature of the workman is an important factor with regard to the fatigue due to working with a barrow. The shortest are at the greatest disadvantage.

Such objective results, say Imbert and Mestre, might be usefully taken into consideration for the regulation of women's and children's barrow-work, and, if a strike were to break out in connection with such labour, we should find, in the literature of the subject, some new points by which to judge the fairness of the worker's claims and for the equitable solution of the dispute. The principle of registration is besides of very general application ; all industrial machinery can be provided with a similar register allowing of the registration of muscular effort.

Professor R. Lépine,[1] of Lyons, after mentioning Imbert's writings, adds, " Once more, such investigations are still only in their infancy, but one can easily guess their destiny ; and in any case, one must admire those who have attempted them, for having shewn that, side by side with the great questions which have until now taken the lead in social medicine, such as tuberculosis, alcoholism, insanity and tenements, there are others, more important in the future, since their solution depends largely on the organisation of labour."

Imbert [2] has also made a study of another kind of labour which consists in spreading out the long branches of American vines in slips of a predetermined length and breadth. This work only occupies a minimum number of people. At Montpellier, for instance, the staff employed never exceeds one hundred, and is almost entirely made up of women and girls. After having made an estimate of this work in mechanical units, it was possible for the present writer to fix, numerically, the amount of work exacted from each worker in return for each centime of her wages. He has thus introduced a new element

[1] R. Lépine, *L'évolution de la Médecine* à *la fin du XIX siecle* (*Revue du Mois*, No. 12, 1906).

[2] Imbert, *Etude expérimentale du travail professionnel ouvrier* (*Revue d'économie politique,* 1909).

into the problem of the general relation which may exist between the wage paid and the labour supplied.

This work, which lasts only for four or five months in the year, from November to March, is carried on either in huge sheds or in the open air ; it begins at 7 a.m., and ends at about 5 p.m., generally with two intervals of rest, one at 8 a.m. for breakfast, the other at noon for the chief meal of the day. As this work is paid by contract and the task of each woman is absolutely independent of that of her companions, each one is absolutely free to regulate her hours of rest according to her own wishes, or even to add to them.

The effects of the cutting were registered by means of graphic inscription. Thanks to the employment of Marey's drum, some of the tracings of muscular effort could be registered. These tracings were calibrated in kilogramme-metres. For each centime of wage the woman had to supply 686 kilogramme-metres of labour. The payment for 1,000 slips was 65 centimes. The women, questioned as to the feelings of fatigue experienced by them, complained of pain in the line of the right shoulder when arranging their hair in the morning. The statements, emanating as they did from working women well accustomed

to work, were evidence that the muscles used
during their work were daily submitted to a
certain amount of over-strain, since the night's
rest was not sufficient for their restoration to a
perfectly normal condition by the following
morning.

With regard to the localisation of the pains
complained of, this is explained by the fact that
for the rather thick slips the sections could not
be cut by the sole action of the flexors of the
fingers which surround the pruning-shears and
thus render the hand immovable ; the fore-arm
is in a certain degree of flexion with regard to
the arm, and hence the cutting is achieved by the
action of the extensor muscles of the fore-arm,
with the fixing of the arm due to the action of
the muscles of the shoulder. It may be noticed
that the over-work of which the women complained
is explained, not by a muscular phenomenon,
properly so-called, as the women did not complain
of any diminution in their power of working,
but by a phenomenon of a nervous order. This
proof shews plainly the importance of the element
of pain in the complex phenomenon of fatigue.

The author also verifies the superiority of some
workwomen over others. Even in an industry
which would seem to belong to those essentially
mechanical, the ability of the worker, and there-

fore his wage, may depend far more on his mental than on his physical qualities. Now, all the details by which the technique of a clever workwoman may be distinguished from that of a mediocre one, are translated in practice into an economy of time in the performance of the various actions which go to the preparation of the slips.[1] And a not less interesting thing is that the mediocre workwoman, who has the same incentive as her more skilled companion to increase her wage, was incapable of recognising and then of imitating those technical details, some of which are moreover very easy to discover.

In other experiments the same writer[2] studied the work of a filer, and determined the characteristics of a good and a bad filer.

We will quote another experiment made by Imbert [3] on transport by means of the common wheelbarrow—a vehicle possessing one wheel only. As the load is generally a low one, the effort to support it is greater than is the case with the *two-wheeled barrow*, and the fatigue is more pronounced. It is in discharging a load of 21 kilogrammes that

---

[1] Imbert, *Exemples d'étude physiologiques directe du travail professionnel ouvrier* (*Revue d'Hygiene et de Police samitaire*, Août, 1909).

[2] A. Imbert, *Les Méthodes de laboratoire appliquees à l'étude directe et pratique des questions ouvriers. Revue général des sciences*, 30 Juin, 1911.

[3] A. Imbert, *Bulletin de l'Inspection du travail*, 1909, Nos. 1 and 2.

the wheelbarrow has advantages over the two-wheeled variety. A load of 21 kilogrammes, directly borne, is the economic limit of a workman's carrying power. Pushing a one-wheeled barrow is more tiring than pushing one with two wheels. It causes a more accentuated action of the respiratory and of the circulatory organs and produces muscular pain, chiefly in the arms, of a more lasting nature than that brought on by wheeling a two-wheeled barrow.

These enquiries most certainly constitute a new and most interesting chapter in social medicine. The Political Economy Section of the French Association for the Advancement of the Sciences (session of 1908 held at Clermont-Ferrand), as well as the IX Congress held at Paris in 1900, by the Working Men's Association for Hygiene and the Safety of Workers, and the 11th International Congress for Industrial Accidents (Rome, 1909), have each, as a result of the outcome of enquiries on the subject, expressed a wish that an immediate experimental study of industrial labour should be encouraged and spread.

Imbert [1] expressed a wish to see workmen take part in Scientific Congresses where questions relating to their work, their food, and the acci-

[1] A. Imbert, *Role des ouvriers dans certains congres scientifiques* (*La Grande Revue*, 10 April, 1909).

dents to which labour was liable, were discussed. They could thus provide a quantity of most useful information.

J. M. Lahy [1] made some experiments among gem-engravers, with a view to discovering signs of technical superiority, and amongst industries demanding well directed rapid action, and voluntary attention—short and intense (electricians for example). He studied the times of nervous reaction, and discovered amongst these men, a constant opposition between the times of their visual, and their auditory, reactions. The first-class worker shows more rapid visual and slower auditory reactions than the less skilled operator. Ch. Richet and Laugier [2] have furnished interesting studies on the same subject.

We cannot pass over in silence Lahy's valuable investigations on the psycho-physiology of the gunner, nor those of de Marchoux, Camus, and Nepper on the aviation candidates, as well as those undertaken by Pierre Menard on the

[1] J. M. Lahy, *L'Adaptation organique dans les états d'attention volontaires et brefs. C.R. de l'Acad. des Sciences*, May, 1913 ; *Les signes physiques de la supérorité professionnelle chez les dactylographes.* Ibid, 2 June, 1913 ; *Etude expér de l'adaptation psycho-physiologiques aux actes volontaires brefs et intenses. Journal de Psychologie*, 1913, pp. 220-236. *Les Conditions psycho-physiologiques de l'aptitude au travail dactylographique. Journal de Physiologie*, 5 July, 1913.

[2] Ch. Richet and H. Laugier, *C.R. de la Soc. de Biologie.* 19 April, 1913.

arterial pressure of soldiers in the trenches.   All
these researches demonstrate variations in human
reactions, a difference in aptitudes, whence comes
the necessity for selection in order to obtain the
best return.

II

THE PRINCIPLES OF SCIENTIFIC MANAGEMENT.

I.—TAYLOR'S STUDIES ON THE ORGANIZATION OF LABOUR.

It is still only a short time ago that the question of the organization of labour from the scientific point of view was first promulgated. The essays cited above had succeeded only in raising the question, without in any way solving it. The problem may be very clearly summed up in a few words,—find the conditions of work which will permit of the workman producing the maximum effective result with a minimum production of fatigue. And we can partially foresee the possibility of solving the problem ; thanks to the scientific methods already in force in the vast domain of the science of labour. Thus, when the echoes of the brilliant success of Taylor's methods, which had rapidly attained celebrity in America, reached Europe, it gave rise to some anxiety.

The workmen who follow these methods rapidly, become twice, three times, even four

times as productive as they originally were.
Let us take some examples. At the *Bethlehem
Steel Company* each man was able to load, daily,
metal moulds, the total weight of which amounted
to 12½ tons. Taylor succeeded in raising this
number to 47 tons. The work consists in laying
hold of a metal mould 42 kilogrammes in weight,
and of setting it down a few paces further off.
This is how Taylor set about increasing the output.
He had first of all made some preliminary experiments on the *speed* and *duration* of human
labour.

Having then found two very strong and good
workmen, he gave them double wages during
the whole time of his experiments, whilst re-
quiring from them their maximum effort and ready
service under strict discipline. These men were
called upon to perform the most diverse tasks.
The times required for each of their movements
was chronographed by means of a time counter.
Thus, it was proved that man can, under these
conditions, daily perform a task varying from
34,000 to 140,000 kilogramme-metres, thus
demonstrating that there is no hard and fast
relation between labour, of whatever kind, and
fatigue, and, on the other hand, that it was necessary to *select* the workmen. It recognised the
necessity of eliminating all slow and useless

movements and of grouping the most rapid and effective movements.

To return to the example quoted, Taylor, in collaboration with Barth, established the fact that a man should only be required to load during a strictly defined time—say 43% of the day, and the 57% remainder of the day he should have his hands empty. But he might be worked 58% of the day if he were called upon to fill half moulds of 22 kilogrammes. And finally, there exists a *loading limit* which he could sustain throughout the day without fatigue. It is thus, that, in superintending the duration of movements, and in eliminating those that were useless, Taylor succeeded in loading 47 tons of metal moulds instead of 12½ tons per man, per day. This work is equivalent to the loading of 1,156 moulds of about 41 kilogrammes each, during 252 minutes ; thus giving a period of 13·07 seconds per mould.

There is, in these experiments, a confirmation of the information collected by Coulomb, Chauveau, Mosso, and Imbert regarding the evaluation of output, and on the economic methods of the work of the human motor. It would appear that most of these writings were unknown to the American engineer, and that he was solely inspired by Coulomb's system. He also had

occasion to testify to the enormous amount of
fatigue produced by *static labour*, often unproductive, for which he had no use, and which he
tried to eliminate.

A second example may be taken from brick-
laying. According to Gilbreth, who collaborated
with Taylor, for handling piles of bricks, a load
must not exceed 40 kilogrammes for a strong man
(first-class) ; 27-31 kilogrammes for a second-
class man. The bricks and the mortar are placed
by an assistant within reach of the brick-layer's
hand ; the latter should confine himself absolutely to placing them ; the top of the brick
being on a level with the hand, the movement
takes place, following the action of the weight,
without contraction. The pile of bricks should
be at the required height so that the layer need
not stoop to pick them up or to work ; his
assistant should carry the bricks on a two-wheeled
barrow, which would allow of the transport of
216 bricks instead of only 60 (a one-wheeled barrow)
etc. By this method, three times as much work
is accomplished.

The example in the office of *Industrial Engineer-
ing* [1] is not less significant. The employees
folded, sealed, and dispatched 20,000 letters per

day. The effect of working according to scientific rules produced the result that the work was accomplished four times as quickly as before. One of the girls succeeded in stamping from 100 to 120 envelopes per minute. She piled up the letters so as to shew the addresses ; the stamps were divided into strips, so as to follow one another horizontally—not vertically. She fixed a small damp sponge to the first finger of her right hand, and, taking a strip of stamps in the same hand, damped them whilst removing them with the thumb and stuck them on the addressed envelopes, the thumb managing to wet the stamps and to separate them from the strip ; and the letters being allowed to fall, by their weight, into a conveniently placed basket.

Taylor's work [1] was made known in France by M. Henri Le Châtelier, Inspector General of Mines, Professor at the Sorbonne, and at the Ecole Supérieure des Mines, who caused his book on the principles of scientific management to be translated into French, and himself wrote the preface to it. He also wrote a preface to Jules Amar's book, already quoted, which devotes a large space to the methods of American engineers. Technical phenomena which appear quite simple are, M. Le Châtelier says, extremely complex ; thus,

[1] Taylor, F. W., *Scientific Management, Harper and Brothers.*

the working of metals on a lathe, of which Taylor
made a special study, depends upon at least
twelve independent variables. Of these variables
the human factor is by far the most important.
It is upon this special point, hitherto hardly
taken into consideration, that Taylor has concentrated his chief attention. We must first
get rid of a very widespread prejudice. People
say that good workmen themselves know how to
use their strength to the best advantage. This
is a mistake, as Taylor has proved by the example
of the transport of loads. In that labour, fatigue
is the result of five variables, and it is impossible
for the workman to discover the relative values
of each of these variables by his sensations. In
studying this problem, Taylor has succeeded in
tripling the weight daily transported by the
workman without adding to his fatigue.

A series of articles was recently devoted by the
Revue de Metallurgie to the works of Frederic
W. Taylor. The first of these articles signed by
M. H. Le Châtelier [1] is written for the purpose of
bringing the scientific character of the system
into notice.

The name of F. W. Taylor, says Le Châtelier,
will be famous in the history of industrial progress
by three great discoveries : (1) The rapid cutting

[1] Le Châtelier, *Frederic Winslow Taylor* (1856-1915).
Revue de Métallurgie, April 1915, pp. 185-232.

of steel ; (2) Regulations for the working of metals ; (3) The principles for the scientific organisation of factories.

It is with this third discovery that we are going to deal here, and to analyse Le Châtelier's article. The essential principle of Taylor's system is the systematic application of the scientific method in the study of industrial phenomena. He begins with an exhaustive enumeration of *all* the factors upon which each phenomenon depends, of each operation to be studied, then, after having recognised all the factors at stake, he decides, by experiments and observations as precisely as possible, the *numerical relations* existing between the different facts brought forward. Taylor was thus brought to the establishment of a certain number of rules collectively known under the name of Taylor's system.

One of the essential items in the cost price of an article is the daily output of the worker. This output depends upon two very important things : the determination of the worker to produce as much as he can and his productive capacity. The workman frequently purposely limits his output because he is afraid of having his wages reduced by his master, and, on the other hand, he realises that his master, more often than not, does not know how much work he can normally accomplish. The remedy for these two motives for idleness is to establish by exact measurements the workman's normal output, and to exact a definite task from him. One of the essential points in the system is the creation of a special department for the fixing of the *normal task*. Moreover, *premiums* may be allotted for the accomplishment of the normal task. Amongst the premium systems, is the *bonus system*, invented by Gantt. The workman's wages are divided into two quite distinct parts : a daily wage, which the workman is sure to receive in any case, and whatever his daily output may be. In addition he receives a fixed premium, called " bonus," when he accomplishes, in the day, the total amount of the task which has been pointed out to him as normal. The foremen, on their side, receive a premium for each workman working under their orders, who earns his premium.

The capacity of a workman's production depends on many circumstances, and particularly on the nature of the materials placed at his disposal. Hence the necessity for having an office for the especial study of the best methods of working. These methods should be known to the men. Therefore, it is also necessary to have another office for the training of overseers capable of guaranteeing this *desideratum*.

F. W. Taylor (born in 1856, died in 1915), was descended from a Philadelphia family ; he was, by turns, apprentice, labourer, master mechanic, then director of a training college, and finally, in 1884, Chief Engineer of the Midvale factories. He took his diploma at the Stevens Institute of Technology. In 1890, he left the Midvale steelworks to become General Director of the Manufacturing Investment Company which manufactured mills for the great chemical industries. He left this Company in 1893, and dedicated the whole of his time to the introduction of his system of organisation into various industries. F. W. Taylor, says M. Le Châtelier, was not only a genius, but he was a man of a noble nature, faithful to his friends, devoted to the public good, and in great sympathy with the aspirations of the working classes. Since Taylor's death, an International Committee has been formed for continuing the struggle on behalf of the American engineer's ideas. The active members of the committee are : Mr. Carl Barth, consulting engineer ; Mr. Norris Cooke, director of public works in the city of Philadelphia ; Mr. Dodge, president of the Link Belt Co. of Philadelphia, whose factories are entirely reorganised on Taylor's plans ; Mr. Hathaway, director of the Tabor Manufacturing Co., Philadelphia ; one of

the first factories to adopt Taylor's methods,
and where those engineers, who go to the United
States to study Taylor's system, are sent. The
secretary of the committee is Miss Frances
Mitchell, Boxly, Highland Station, Chestnut Hill,
Philadelphia, U.S.

Let us now examine Taylor's system closely,
basing our enquiries on those of M. Le Châtelier·
The complete enumeration of all the determining
conditions of no matter what phenomenon, is,
in Taylor's opinion, of capital importance. One
does not *a priori* take account of the fact, he says,
that all the work of the engineer is rendered
useless if the smallest doubt exists as to one of these
conditions. Now, workmen do not take systematic
note of the determining conditions of their
operations.

Besides, one must know how to measure
the dimensions of the phenomenon under observation, as, for example, the distinctive mechanical
qualities of a certain steel, the expenditure of
energy in the rolling, etc.

It is thus that Taylor succeeds in establishing
the most economical conditions in labour. One of
the experimental methods systematically employed
by Taylor is that of *Chronography*. Time is
one of the essential elements in the cost price of
all individual effort ; it must therefore, be measured

like the other factors. This operation occupies a prominent place in the system, more important than those of other elements by reason of the double part it plays : first of all, it helps in the study of experiments ; and it is also the necessary foundation of the system for the payment of the workman.

One form of Chronography is the application of cinematography to the analysis of very rapid movements, which would escape observations made by the naked eye. One of Taylor's disciples, Mr. Gilbreth, has gone back to Marey's chrono-photographic process, placing on the worker's hand, whilst he works, a small incandescent lamp so as to show his movements by a shaft of light. This method goes by the name of cyclegraph.

M. Le Châtelier says, quite rightly, that, in spite of all these efforts, these attempts all still show a most important gap,—the fatigue of the worker is not measured. We are referred back to his declarations. Physiologists will, before long, be able to give us experimental methods, on this point, suited to industrial research.

Not satisfied with the results of these experiments, Taylor took a lot of trouble to translate them by means of algebraic formula.

The difference, therefore, between Taylor's method and that of other engineers is as follows :

let us take a particular example, that of leather belts. According to M. Le Châtelier, before Taylor's time, a lot of experiments had already been made with leather belts—chiefly with regard to measuring their tenacity. But tenacity is not the only quality needed for the good working of leather belts. It is only after having tabulated the speeds of these belts, the frequency of greasing, their gradual elongation during use, the number of times they fall, and the length of the stoppages thus caused in the work of the shops, that Taylor was able to give the scientific solution of the problem, that is to say, to define the conditions under which the maximum service is obtained with the minimum expenditure.

Amongst the factors of productivity, workmanship is certainly the most important.

The capricious behaviour of human motive-power would seem to place this element outside all law, and enable it to escape the control of science, says Le Châtelier. Taylor has demonstrated that the laws discovered by experiments of this nature, and which correspond to the very complex organisation of the human being are subject to a larger number of exceptions than the laws relating to material things. That, however, laws of that kind do exist, which apply to the great majority of people, and which, clearly defined, are a great help in guiding them, we give the following example. Wishing to know the best plan to adopt in reprimanding a workman, Taylor said, that the preference should be given to a fine, without any reproach, the importance of the fine being in proportion to the gravity of the offence. That was the most efficacious plan of action, and at the same time, the least disagreeable. Certain precautions should, however, be taken. The fines should, in no case, be entered in the Principal's cash book, but should go towards supporting some fund, by which the workers benefited—towards insurance against accidents, by preference.   In this department, measurement cannot be as precise, as in the case of machinery ; it is necessary to draw up statistics, to adopt measures.   The psychology of the working man does not appear in our instructions.   The expenses incurred by these enquiries are largely repaid by the increase in productivity.

From these investigations connected with *experimental science*, M. Le Châtelier passes on to the *Psychology of the Workingman and the organisation of labour,* following Taylor's plan. *Scientific Management* includes both scientific experiment and its particular application to the human factor. Here are the essential points of his teaching :—

E

1. It is incorrect to believe, as the politicians of all countries try to represent, that the workman is a stupid creature, deaf to all intelligent reasoning. According to Taylor, psychology of the working man in no way differs from that of other men.

2. With modern methods of work, which are very perfect, but also very complicated, it is no longer possible for the workman to discover by intuition, in each particular case, the most advantageous movements of the hand. Their settlement, in the present day, rests with the principals— the engineers. It is folly, though it is still often done, to place a workman before a lathe and require him to find out himself how to make the best use of it. That best depends, as Taylor has shewn, upon a dozen different things. It took him twenty-five years to disentangle the most advantageous combinations ; how could a working man, in a few minutes, divine the solution of such a complicated problem ? It is, therefore, indispensable to separate the preparation of the work,—an essentially intellectual process,—from its accomplishment, an essentially manual labour. According to Taylor, the methods employed

in a workshop should be entirely regulated by a special technical staff, and then taught to the workmen by the same staff. Therein lies an entire revolution in our industrial methods; very few engineers would possess the actual knowledge necessary for studying their workmen's processes, and fewer still the ability necessary, to put them into practice before them.

3. Another very important result of Taylor's studies has to do with the great advantage of piece-work. The workman sees the exact amount of work accomplished each day ; the size of the task is regulated according to information furnished by previous experience, with a view to determining the best working conditions.

4. This change in the organisation of labour imposes considerable effort and expense on the management of the factory. But it exacts nothing more from the workman ; less initiative on the one hand, more discipline on the other, but not more physical fatigue. But, as these methods considerably augment the production of each workman, the owner is in a position to increase the wages. The assent of the workman is obtained by an increase in wage rising

from 30 to 100% of the mean rate of wages.
The adoption of these principles will permit
of the doubling or trebling of the production.
So that this organisation may be possible,
an *office for the preparation and distribution
of the work* in the workshops receives the
manager's orders and distributes them to the
right workshops.   The regulation of piece-work
involves the necessity of a new organisation—
that of statistics.   All this necessitates a very
numerous staff; the number of clerks is increased,
that of the workmen diminished.   That is the
outcome of the organisation of labour, according
to Taylor's system.

The *social consequences* of this system are
studied at the close of M. Le Châtelier's article.
These consequences have given rise to numerous
controversies.   The principal criticisms brought
forward are :—

1. The increase in production, the essential
   purpose of Taylor's system, can only be
   obtained by over-working the men ;
2. The workman is brought down to the level of
   a machine, his intellectual and social
   position is lowered ;
3. The monotony of the work, and the absence
   of all intellectual effort, discourages skilled
   workmen.

To these objections, Le Châtelier replies.
Taylor's system does not increase, but reduces
over-work ; this is the opinion of all those who
have seen it in operation. The increased production is entirely due to regulations independent
of the workman's actions ; a better supervision
of the machinery and belting, a more regular
supply of the materials, the employment of
better tools, etc. It is, moreover, incorrect to
say, that the rate of mortality amongst the
workmen is higher than heretofore, as Phila-
delphian statistics shew when compared to
those of Paris.

The assertion that the workman is brought
down to the level of a machine is incorrect in
every particular ; it is the dexterous movements
employed in Taylor's method which results in
producing the skilled workman.

Another sentimental objection, says Le Châtelier,
may seem more specious. It is sad to see the
artistic workman disappear—the man capable of
exercising all the branches of his calling, of
working in stone, in wood, and in metal, and of
producing such works of art as adorn our Gothic
churches. Why then, not regret the slaves of
antiquity ? (Le Châtelier). Did not they build
magnificent palaces, temples, and mausoleums,
which to this day arouse our admiration ? This is

true, but the artisans of the Middle Ages dwelt in
kennels, without air or light, were badly fed and
liable to epidemics. To-day, the working man
has a healthy home, is often as well fed as his
employer, etc. The specialisation of work and
the employment of machinery have given him
all these good things. In the course of a century
his wealth has increased ten-fold. Taylor invites
him to double this again, and people want to oblige
him to decline this gift out of respect to a few
rather antiquated principles. On the contrary,
progress will consist in more intensive methods of
production, in reducing the length of the working
day—to an eight hours' day at once, later on,
perhaps, to a six hours' day.

It is untrue to assert that specialisation, and
the constant repetition of the same work disgusts
the men. That is to contradict our daily experience, says Le Châtelier. What more monotonous than the calling of a forwarding agent,
or even that of the head employé in a big firm ?
And yet the number of candidates for such berths
is enormous, and those privileged to hold them
are the objects of envy. Then, the farm labourer, each day following the furrows of his
plough, does not question the monotony of his
work. All his life-long he repeats the process,
without being any the worse. According to the

experience of competent heads of industries, it would be just the same with workmen. Hardly will you find one in a hundred capable of realising the monotony of his work. The workman performs his work without thinking about it, quietly dreaming about his own little affairs, his plans, etc. (see our criticisms below).

To wind up, Le Châtelier maintains that Taylor's system will advance more rapidly in the future. The slowness of its development is due to the necessity for perfect accord between the masters and the foreman of the workshops before it can be got into working order. At present, for two men, both imbued with new doctrines to meet in the same factory, is rare.

The second article published by the *Revue de Métallurgie*, is that by C. B. Thomson,[1] Professor at Harvard University, on the *Scientific Organization of Labour*, he summarises the principal publications issued up to now, on Taylor's system and gives numerous examples of its industrial application.

This bibliography by itself forms quite a literature, and includes articles on the theory of scientific management, on its action, its scientific organisation, on railways, on methods, on the human factor in scientific organisation, and on work-

[1] Revue de Métallurgie, Vol. XII, April 1915 pp. 233-315.

men's syndicates. The most important are those by Taylor himself, notably his *Principles of Scientific Management* and *Shop Management*, as well as his *Art of Cutting Metals*. He draws attention to the prejudice which permits in believing that the improvement in the methods of labour will reduce the number of workmen employed in the industry. This was the complaint at one time urged against machinery, yet no one would now abolish the latter. It will be the same with scientific management, the improvements in working methods only bringing passing inconveniences in their train, when developed too rapidly, causing profound disturbance in the existing economic conditions.

Thomson thus sums up (according to Kendall), the processes which unite in increasing the workman's output.

1. *Elementary Analysis of Operations.*—This systematic study allows of the elimination of useless movements, of the combination of the most advantageous movements, of modifying certain imperfections in the machinery.

For example, in a factory for lighting apparatus, it sufficed to carry the pieces to be manipulated to the operator, arranged in a box, and placed 20 centimetres from his left hand, in order to perceptibly increase his output ; until then, his pieces had been scattered higgledy piggledy round him.

2. *Selection of Workmen.*—Workmen differ greatly in their aptitude for the same work. These differences may be sufficient to shew a variation of 50% in their output. To take book-binding as an example, it will be granted that a big, strong girl is best suited for the carrying of heavy parcels of books, whilst for gilding, one with very delicate, careful fingers should be chosen.

3. *Training of Workmen.*—The workman has to be taught the improved methods.

4.—*The Employment of Good Tools.*

5. *Stimulants.*—The workman is incited, by means of a premium which increases his wage, to supply as large an output, as the implements placed at his disposal will permit of.

According to Carlton's opinion (quoted by Mr. Thomson), up to this point, the scientific management of labour has only taken the point of view of one of the parties interested into account ; to succeed, it is absolutely necessary that, from the start, there should be complete accord between the masters and men, and this accord can only be obtained by accepting the intervention of

syndicates, and by admitting workmen's delegates
into the Councils of the management.

The following are the other articles in *La
Revue de Métallurgie : Annual Report* by M.
M. L. Cooke, which shews the services rendered
by Taylor's method in the administration of a
large town ; Mr. Renold's memorandum on the
*Scientific Management of Factories (l'Organisation
scientifique des usines) ;* that by Mr. Allingham
on the same subject, and finally, that by Mrs.
Christine Frederiks relating to the *scientific
management of a house.* Scientific methods may
also benefit domestic life. The first thing to be
considered is the standardisation of the required
movements . Movements should be regulated,
Mrs. Frederiks pleads, even in the washing of
dishes. It is useless to lift plates from right to
left by crossing one arm over the other. Every-
thing one does should be examined so as to settle
what is essential and to see if it answers its purpose
properly, and without annoyance to the operator.
The authoress made use of these methods when
organising her model kitchen at Applecroft.
She gives the principles upon which she grouped
her utensils in relation to the place where they
would be used and with reference to their normal
use. Secondly, there comes that very important
question—*the fixing of a normal time-table.* A

list would facilitate the daily and weekly tasks, etc.

Finally, the normalisation of purchases, of the staff, and of management, have their allotted place.

The article is most interesting, and contains any amount of excellent advice having for its end the scientific organisation of that most important side of life, the home of the family.

The only objection which we can make to the system is that the mistress of the house must, herself, be able to direct the work required, no matter what it may be. This specialization in such a number of departments would become too onerous for the mistress and would confine her absolutely to the sphere of the house to the exclusion of all other interests ; it is besides opposed to the evolution of the family in modern society, an evolution which tends to eliminate a host of functions from house management, and to make co-operative duties of those which used to devolve on the house mistress alone. But there is nothing to be said against the various groups—co-operatives for example, whose spheres extend beyond the narrow limits of a family profiting by these Councils. Also, family life itself should be Taylorised in the sense of order, economy and better management.

2.—THE OPINION THAT SHOULD BE FORMED OF
THE PRINCIPLES OF SCIENTIFIC MANAGEMENT.

To resume, after this account, our personal
opinion as to Taylor's system. This system is
most certainly indisputably scientific in character,
and all those who desire, henceforth, to study the
organisation of labour, will be unable to ignore
his system. He came at the right time, and
although Taylor was ignorant of much of the
scientific work which had been accomplished
in the physiological laboratories of Europe,
thanks to his personal experiences he achieved
distinct results, of which many are only a confirmation of general laws established by scientific
research. It seems certain that from the
technological point of view, he was entirely
successful, and the proof lies in the enormous
augmentation of production which he was, in
almost every case, able to obtain. This is no
small result, and it is indisputably true. But
here our eulogy ends. To praise Taylor's system
and to desire its general introduction into the
industrial world one would have to feel sure on
many points, of which several are still obscure,
and others are debatable, if not to be condemned.
Certain it is that the scientific management of

labour is an inevitable necessity, but it remains to be proved whether Taylor's system, the first to be advocated in this field of enquiry, is just the very best system, that which was impatiently awaited by all those who wished to see science penetrate into the region of industrial labour, in order that it might be reorganised for the great benefit of society.

From our point of view, we can charge Taylor's system with three great faults :—

1. As the most convinced partisans of Taylor's system affirm, a big gap exists in Taylor's estimates, which is the absence of scientific information concerning the fatigue of the workers. Such information as does exist depends upon the statements of the workers, which are unreliable. This gap may be imagined ; the calculation of fatigue is a very delicate process and can only be attempted by physiologists trained in such studies. Now, that was the first thing that should have been done, seeing that Taylor's system upsets the usual habits, changes the movements, quickens them in some cases, and imprints upon the human motor an absolutely new action. It is not enough that, in certain cases, this factor has been taken into consideration. Thus Barth

succeeded in formulating the laws of the relationship between labour and fatigue ; Gilbreth noticed that the two-wheeled barrow causes less fatigue, because it is better balanced, than the one-wheeled barrow, etc. But, as Le Châtelier says, these statements are insufficient. In his book, *The Human Motor*, Amar also considers that Taylor's method is insufficient from the physiological point of view, the learned American not having had the means by which to estimate the amount of fatigue, to know the speed, the rhythm, the effort which are exacted by even the smallest expenditure of energy, in a maximum of labour. And yet, a few pages below, Amar asserts that " the art of working is thus constituted and firmly established on scientific foundations." As a matter of fact, this assertion goes far beyond the facts, the question of fatigue being essential and the charge of overwork having been, in a great number of cases, brought against Taylor and his disciples.

With a view to solving this problem, an International Committee made up partly of physiologists and partly of engineers, and of absolutely independent sociologists appointed by a recognised official Institution of repute should be charged with the examination of fatigue amongst men employed in the various industries that have adopted Taylor's system. It is only after enquiry, and in the event of a favourable answer, that Taylor's system will deserve the name of " scientific," and may be considered to be free from all defect.

2. This system offers no guarantee to the workman in that which relates to his own advantage. It is true that, at the present time, the workman enjoys a rise in wage and a reduction in his hours of work, when he adopts Taylor's system, but it is to be feared that when everybody is working under this system of scientific management, these advantages may suddenly cease. The fear of general discontent, say even a strike, might not suffice to insure the continuance of the increased wages. Therefore, here again, some reform is required, and it is necessary as Carlton (quoted by Thomson), insists that workmen's syndicates should take part in the councils of the management.

3. The theory of " premiums," which is part of the system itself, makes it probable that, to a certain extent, over-work is almost sure to prevail. In order to urge the workman to produce his maximum output Taylor makes use of too strong a stimulant, an infallible one even, that of direct gain attached to increased labour. As the feeling of fatigue is not irrevocable, and may be concealed by increased effort, the workman may rapidly reach the limits of over-pressure and be unaware of it until the moment when, quite exhausted and good for nothing, he is turned out of the factory which had dazzled him with visions of the most extraordinary and attractive benefits. This reproach has been formulated against Taylor's system of scientific management, many times, by its adversaries (" the premium of over-pressure ").

The principles of this system are, moreover, opposed to those of the progress of hygiene, which tends to become more and more general even in the case of individuals. This freedom of the individual to overwork, is opposed to eugenics and to all those sciences which have for their aim the betterment of the race. Finally, the reward to those who work the best is not a proceeding to be advocated from the moral point of view, for those who are trained on such a principle make it the mainspring of their actions under other conditions.

Such are the fundamental faults of the system, and doubtless many others would be discovered in it, were it to be examined on the spot. On the other hand, we think many of the attacks levelled against the system are worthless. " It degrades the human being, because of the monotony of the mechanical actions which it enforces," etc. That is an argument of the ignorant and merits no attention. Neither can the monotony of the work itself, and the absence of any intellectual element, be considered as criticisms. Le Châtelier refutes such charges, but we cannot, in this matter, agree with his point of view. It is clear that his example of the rate of mortality amongst the workmen in Philadelphia being no higher than in Paris, is no argument. On the other hand, if one does not regret the abolition of slavery (see p. 69), that is not solely on account of the unhealthy conditions under which the slaves lived, but chiefly on account of the conditions under which the work was performed (labour " by compulsion "). With regard to the objection to the employment of forwarding agent, or of the office clerk, it is in the bitter struggle for existence,

F

and in the fact that many men are unqualified
for any other form of employment, that the
true reasons nust be looked for to account for
the number of applicants for these posts, and not
in any love of monotonous work.

Would that all labour might be as monotonous
as that carried on in the bosom of nature, amidst
its ever changing charms, and its sensations
of life, liberty and beauty.

As a matter of fact, the monotony of labour
is not a reproach that can touch Taylor's system,
any more than the absence of the intellectual
element and the increase of discipline with the
reduction of individuality and spontaneity. The
charge of monotony may be brought against all
manufacturing industries—the monotony only
differs in degree. That fault is irreducible, like
that which relates to the machines themselves.
Industrial labour is, by its very essence, monotonous, and very unintellectual, tending inevitably
towards an ever greater and ever more complete
automatism. The physiologists of industry are
well aware of this. They recognise the difference
between manual labour, such as is taught in the
schools, from the pedagogic point of view, and that
which is performed by the workman, from the
industrial point of view. In the first case, it is a
question of educative action, bringing pressure

to bear on the psycho-motor centres, of which the hand is the only trusty instrument. Also it would seem necessary to vary the nature of the work, in order to bring a larger number of brain cells into play and, as soon as the work becomes easy and begins to become automatic, it should be stopped and something fresh commenced.

It is quite a different question with the workman. He works continuously at the same craft, always the same, which he brings to the greatest possible point of perfection, and his tendency, desire, and aim, is the greatest possible autonomy. To-day, the friends of the people know quite well that industrial labour cannot be a source of mental evolution for the labourer. This conviction urges them to further economise the workman's strength, to reduce his hours of work by improving the work itself, and by giving him the consolation of a healthy home in the country, and a training able to supplement the autonomy demanded by his rôle as an industrial worker, and which the needs of our civilization render absolutely necessary. And it is thus that humanitarian claims, are now, on many points, based on science.

Thus does Taylor's system present itself to the present writer. We have not stripped it of its scientific character, but we do perceive that it exhibits numerous faults and gaps in its conception. Is this system capable of being sufficiently perfected and improved to permit of its some day occupying a leading place in the organisation of labour, or does it, on the contrary, possess fundamental errors, which will prevent its general acceptance, and condemn it to failure ? Ulterior research can alone enable us to answer these questions. However that may be, this system should, at the present hour, claim the attention of manufacturers, and after the actual crisis through which we are now passing is over, and the need for new enterprise and an accelerated productivity makes itself felt, the scientific organisation of labour will become a greater necessity than ever before. One can only regret that, as yet, scientific methods have not given us the decisive answer we seek, and that the solution of the problem, at present, is only empirical. . . In any event, Taylor's system, in spite of its many advantages, should only be applied with great caution and tact, since it is suspected of over-pressure, which may prove harmful to the race.

At the time of going to press with this book, we note the recently published work by J. M. Lahy.[1] This writer advances many objections

---

[1] J. M. Lahy, *Le systeme Taylor et la physiologie du travail professionnel*, Paris 1916, Matton, 198 pages.

to Taylor's system, his conception of labour being spoilt by a threefold error : psychological, sociological, and industrial ; he improves methods, not with a view to the well-being of the workman, but in order to insure the super-production of each. Work, in the factories reorganised according to Taylor's methods, is based upon constraint and discipline, which are the opposites of invention and lead to fatigue ; the workman is only looked upon as part of the system. The abstract question of scientifically determining the worker's fatigue has no place in his system, and in as far as workers are concerned, he pre-assumes them to be idle. The problem of selection, of which Taylor thinks so much, does not really aim at superior workmanship, but only at the result of movements, so that Taylor has not set before each industry the double criterion of superior workmanship with minimum fatigue, though this would be the claim made for really scientific experiments. Taylor's methods shew progress in some respects, but the work is not produced more perfectly, it is only more rapid.[1] It is, after all, the yield of the worker which regulates the duration and intensity of the work, and when all is said and done the results

[1] This greater speed in work, the quality of which is in no respect lowered, is nevertheless a real improvement, but that alone should not satisfy us.

are often disappointing. Taylor employed, for
human labour, the same tests that he used for
mechanical work, which is a mistake, because of
fatigue, which intervenes in the action of the
human motor. His disciples, like himself, only
examined this problem theoretically. Taylor knew
nothing of physiology, his study of motion is
far from being as precise as Marey's.[1] Inventions
said to be by him or his disciples were really
Marey's. His system contains numerous gaps,
it is incomplete, it has not entirely transformed
the organisation of labour ; his system does
take the workman into account, but it leads to
the depreciation of the skilled worker. His
system of wages and premiums is an encouragement to over-production, and consequent over-
fatigue. Of psychic problems, of all that concerns,
for example, the rhythm of labour, and rest,
both essentially individual matters, Taylor was
ignorant. Many industries he did not study

[1] It is not without interest to remember all that we owe to
Marey, the inventor of the *Graphic* method and of *Chromo-
photography*. Lahy reminds us that side by side with his
classical works, known to all physiologists, Marey tried
some experiments on industrial labour, and promoted other
researches in that domain in his laboratory in the *parc des
Princes* or in the Institute that bears his name. More
especially see : E. J. Marey, *Travail de l'homme dans les
professions Manuelles*. Revue d'Hygiene alimentaire, 1904,
p. 197.—Id. *L'économie de travail et l'élasticité*. La Revue
des Idées, 14 May, 1904. Ch. Frémont, *Etude expérimentale
du rivetage*. Soc. d'encouragement pour l'Industrie nationale,
Paris, 1906.

at all. Also, Taylor invented nothing essential, he only improved certain things. The chronography of elementary movements, which is the original idea of the system, is not sufficient and would not be able to replace the terrestial chronography previously in use.

Many of these charges can be substantiated, and we have already stated our opinion on the subject of fatigue. Still, Lahy talks of an increase of fatigue as though it were a proved and indisputable fact. We cannot share his opinion when he pretends that the chronography of elementary movements exacts a degrading submission on the part of the workman which he would not accept. Now, says Lahy, if the various measures so lauded by Taylor are not irrevocably united, we are no longer in the presence of Taylor's system. We consider that Taylor's system is incomplete, many industries have never been studied, the part played by fatigue has not been estimated. That is an undeniable fact. But those who follow Taylor may correct the errors of his system and perfect it. It is, says Le Châtelier,[1] for the physiologists to determine the rôle played by fatigue. Taylor did what he could. Besides, Lahy thinks, too,

[1] J. Amar, *Organisation physiologique du travail*, 1917 Paris, Dunod et Pinat. Preface by M. Le Châtelier.

that in what Taylor did, there was no preconceived intention of over-working the men ; his work was absolutely sincere.

Taylor himself said that scientific management did not necessarily lead to a great invention nor to the discovery of startling new facts ; it consists in a certain combination of elements not yet realized, and in the grouping of analysed and classified ideas in the form of laws and regulations constituting a science.

We will conclude by saying that no political party should derive any benefit from the scientific management of labour, but society as a whole. Taylor's system, completed on some points, improved in others, put into harmony with the distribution of energy and with psychology, will only receive a definite sanction on the day when it puts itself in agreement with the economic organisations of labour, such as the workman's syndicates and the co-operatives.

These problems will continue to be of essential importance until that far distant day when machines will be able to undertake the labour until now accomplished by man. But at the present time all scientific experiments concerning the management of labour agree in according to the " human " factor the preponderating rôle.

3.—THE FUNCTION OF THE SCHOOL IN THE
DETERMINATION OF APTITUDES.

We are still dealing with the same question—
the utilization of labour, and the fatigue it
causes, when we turn our attention to the experiments which, for the last twenty-five years, have
had the child as their object and have led to the
founding of a new department of science,
Pedology (Science of study of the Child). At
the International Congress of Hygiene and
Demography held at Brussels in 1903, I insisted
on a preliminary medical examination of working
men (see above) with the object of gauging their
aptitudes and of guiding them in their choice of a
career. All those who have mistaken their path
in life become an easy prey to over-work ; their
productivity is greatly reduced and, as a consequence, their prosperity. In this unsuitability
for certain occupations may be detected some of
the causes of over-work and social unproductivity.

This point of view has become considerably
more general than it used to be, and the study of
pedology has shewn us the necessity for carrying
back this examination to a much earlier age, of
making it obligatory in preparatory schools or
even earlier still, and of bringing it to bear in

every department of life, physically, intellectually,
and morally. The medico-pedagogic inspection,
such as has been carried out in the schools of most
countries, for some years now, is a step forward
towards the solution of the problem, but will
not be sufficient in itself. The question is,
as a matter of fact, the determining of aptitudes
and inaptitudes, and those which a medical
examination is able to disclose, only constitute
one side of the examination (organs of sense,
growth, physical constitution, maladies, in short
only the authropometric and pathological points
of view). The vast field of intellectual aptitudes,
properly so called, artistic and technical aptitudes,
remains unexplored.

As regards the two first groups we will refer
the reader to our books,[1] previously published
on this subject. As in this chapter we only
propose to deal with the work of the artisan, we
shall only examine aptitudes of a technical order.

[1] See especially : La Revue Psychologique, published by us
since 1908 (Brussels) ; les Travaux du premier Congres
international de Pédologie (the Work of the first international
Congress of Pedology) which met at Brussels in 1911, and
whose two volumes we were instrumental in publishing, as also
the publication of the International Faculty of Pedology
Faculté Internationale de Pédologie) of Brussels. This institution of which we undertook the management is a school for
higher education especially intended for the initiation of
modern teachers into all the sciences and technology of the
child. Subsequent events in Belgium have forced as to close
this institution, but with the firm intention of re-opening
it some day.

The present state of the science of pedology only requires that tentative measurements of a special kind should be taken, not only in the *primary schools*, but also in the *technical schools* (Industrial Training Colleges). The first are intended for those pupils who have not yet chosen a career, and who put out feelers in every direction. It is in these schools that aptitudes are awakened. It is time that the greater or less degree of skill shewn by the pupils during their studies, should serve as a guide to intelligent and competent teachers, but the estimate thus formed is insufficient by itself, and the present progress of science is opposed to a purely empirical opinion. In every domain, empiricism must inevitably be replaced by scientific information. This is a universal law, the realization of which ensures progress. Now, at this moment, there exist a series of measurements, possible experiments by which we can take the measure of all the senses which intervene in the various mechanical actions : *the diverse forms and degrees of tangible sensitiveness*, of *sensitiveness to pressure*, of *the sense of resistance*, of *precision of movements*, of *their speed*, of *the various forms of the kinesthetic sense* (muscular sense). These senses may be described under the general name of " mechanical senses."

Let us to these add *sight*, with all the elements, which includes : *the sense of proportion, sensitiveness to form, colour, light, perspective*. In passing on to the higher psychic qualities, we see the enormous importance of the *power of attention*, of a *technical memory*, and of *mechanical imagination*, where there is a question of invention. One must not ignore the *value* of *design*, of *modelling*, of *wood-carving*, of *sculpture*, and finally of *taste*, and the *aesthetic sense* (decoration), which plays a preponderating part in the art-worker's labours. All these faculties, including those which want of space prevents our enumerating here, may be examined, studied, gauged, and their diverse combinations go to the making of those complicated powers which we call aptitudes. What should we say of a society wherein everyone should have followed the line of his tastes, of his leanings and aptitudes, where each would occupy the place best suited to him, and wherein the various occupations were allotted to the " most apt " ? Such a society would be reformed from top to bottom, in the sense of greater equity, greater productivity, and greater happiness.

This principle of " the most apt " should regulate our society of the future. This principle is not that of equality, but justice is not the equivalent of complete equality. Justice is opposed, in any case, to the extremes of inequality —to real injustice, such as one sees in the present day.

We should like to formulate a second resolution (the first being the scientific examination of Taylor's system), and that is to see that the " science of aptitudes " is taught, forming a chapter in individual experimental psychology, and penetrating into all those institutions whose duty it is to train our technical and industrial workers of the future, as well as the workers in art, and that with the object of discovering real talents and of directing them into those channels which shall be the most favourable to themselves and to society.

III

THE POWER AND APTITUDE FOR WORK.

I.—THE VALUATION OF THE POWER AND WORK OF THE RIGHT HAND AND THE LEFT.

The Anthropometric Comparison of the Sexes.

The problem of right-handedness and left-handedness far surpasses the limits of muscular power ; it constitutes a chapter in cerebral psycho-physiology. But the most noticeable fact, that which in the first blush claims general attention, is certainly the different powers constantly exhibited between the two hands, with the result that most people are " right-handed," and a very insignificant minority " left-handed."

Here, we shall only examine their difference in strength. The following chapters will deal with other points, and, for the various questions touching right-handedness and left-handedness, we will refer the reader to former publications.[1]

[1] J. L. Ioteyko, *Theorie psycho-physiologique de la droiterie ;* Revue philosophique, juin et juillet 1916, and V. Kipiani, *Ambidextrie,* 103 p., Lebèque, Brussels, Alcan, Paris, 1912.

We must remember that asymmetry has not only to do with movement, but also extends to the various sensorial and psychic functions. Thus, Van Biervliet, [1] when experimenting on the students of the University of Ghent, discovered in the muscular sense, in sharpness of vision, and of hearing, and sensitiveness of touch, a degree of asymmetry, which he calculated at *one tenth.*

If, he says, we denote by the number ten the sensitiveness of the more developed side, which is the right side in the case of the right-handed man, and the left in the case of the left-handed) then the number nine will about denote the opposite side.

In passing on to the question of motor-power, we must distinguish between the test of strength and the test of endurance. The first may be reckoned by the *dynamometer*, an instrument that registers the momentary effort of the pressure of the hand. It measures the strength of the person, his power of making a great effort, but does not calculate the endurance. This latter may be estimated by the use of one of the most scientific processes of measurement, namely, Mosso's ergograph, which we ourselves have used in many experi-

---

[1] Van Biervliet, *Bull. de l'Acad. Roy. de Belgique, class: des Sciences,* 1897-1901.

ments whilst studying different conditions of work. The experiment consists in systematically raising (following the beats of a metronome), a weight (from 2-5 kilograms), by means of the flexion of the middle finger. This experiment may be made up to the limit of extreme fatigue. The graphic method allows of the registering of the extent (height) to which it is raised, and an easy calculation (multiply the total height to which it is raised by the weight), gives the amount of mechanical work performed in kilogramme-metres, whilst the time taken to produce complete fatigue is an indication of individual endurance. These two proofs are, therefore, very different in kind, and it would be interesting to make parallel studies of the behaviour of different people in this respect. These comparative experiments have been made in Belgium, a country where the number of left-handed people seems to be considerable ; far in excess of the generally accepted number which is from 2-3%.

As regards the measurement of strength by the dynamometer, my experiments on 140 students of both sexes at the University of Brussels [1] shewed that the stronger side is to the weaker side as 1,000 to 841 and this as much amongst the

[1] J. Ioteyko, *Mesure de la force dynamometrique des deux mains*, amongst 140 students of the Brussels University. Mémoires de la Société d'anthropologie de Bruxelles, 1903-4.

right-handed as the left-handed students, in other words, the figure which we propose to call the *dynamometric sign*, seems to be constant, even though the average of a sufficiently large group of subjects is taken. This average is 51 kilograms for the stronger hand, and 43 kilograms for the weaker.

In this figure we include students of both sexes. The difference between the two sides is, therefore, an average of 16%, when it is a question of the test of strength.

Let us examine some other figures relating to dynamometric power.

Dynamometric Strength of young people of about twenty years of age (Belgian).

Quételet (1834)
{ Right 39. Kg.3
{ Left 37. Kg.2
} Difference between the two hands, 2 Kg.1.

Ioteyko (1903) Students
{ Right 51. Kg.4
{ Left 43. Kg.0
} Difference 8 Kg.4.

Ioteyko (1908) Students in Normal schools
{ Right 52. Kg.0
{ Left 47. Kg.5
} Difference 4 Kg.5.

This table shews several important facts : there has been a marked increase of strength since Quételet's time, which may be set down to a good physical education.

G

In the second place the want of symmetry has also considerably increased, and this is more marked amongst the students of the University than amongst the pupils in the normal schools. The degree of asymmetry also increases with the age of the children ; Schuyten, who verified this fact, is alarmed at it, seeing that it is correlative to an absence of symmetry in all the organs and all the functions.

As regards the power of endurance or of resistance to fatigue some work was done, under our advice, by Schouteden,[1] who experimented on 18 male and 7 female students in the Brussels University—pupils in our course of experimental psychology. The interesting thing is, that the product of mechanical work of the two sides (*ergographic sign*) is the same amongst the right-handed and left-handed workers, if the general average is taken. By including the 25 cases in a common measure, a difference of 20% is obtained in favour of the stronger side (4 kilogrammes 562, and 3 kilogrammes 246).

The result of these experiments is that the degree of asymmetry is not identical for these different tests.

It is 10% lower for the various senses (muscular,

[1] H. Schouteden, *Ergographie de la Main droite et de la main gauche*. Annales de la Société Roy. des Sciences Niéd. et nat. de Bruxelles, XIII, 1904.

tactile, visual and auditory). It rises markedly in the test of strength to 16% ; and it mounts at a considerable and disproportionate rate in the test of endurance or resistance to fatigue viz., 29%. The table below represents these results.

Bi-manual index (degrees of asymmetry)
(STUDENTS).

Table Sensorial Index — Sensitiveness of touch ,, ,, muscle ,, ,, sight ,, ,, hearing — difference Van Biervliet 10%

Index of Strength   J. Ioteyko   16%

Index of Resistance to fatigue   H. Schouteden 29%
(Endurance)

We will not generalise on these results ; the different co-efficients may vary according to circumstances, but it seems probable that the tendency of the phenomena would remain the same.

This difference of strength and of endurance, between the two hands, is, therefore, very considerable amongst even students who do no manual work. And we must not lose sight of the fact that this is only one method [1] by which, in certain cases, individual differences may

[1] Van Biervliet alone asserts that the bilateral relation of sensibilities remains constant for each individual, even.

acquire a much higher rate. Those who have made experiments of this nature must often have been struck by the inert aspect of the left hand, in the case of many people. Besides, they say : " I can do nothing with that hand ! that doesn't count."

In our opinion, these results should be verified by the examination of the strength and powers of endurance amongst artisans in different industries, in those which require the use of only one hand and in those which are ambidextrous. We should thus obtain a better utilisation of physical aptitudes. We might even go in for individual training, and, by suitable exercises, correct any excessive asymmetry.

We will now compare the degree of muscular asymmetry amongst men and amongst women.

According to Klippel, Pitres, Ferrari, d'Almeida de Roche, etc., the woman has a greater tendency towards the equalisation of the two sides, which may even lead to the predominance of the left hand. It is for that reason that Klippel calls the right cerebral hemisphere, the feminine brain, and the left cerebral hemisphere, the masculine brain. D'Almeida de Roche considers that woman is functionally left-handed, whilst man is right-handed. Under the influence of great fatigue, produced by a protracted use of the ergograph, the predominance of the right side in man, and of the left side in woman, clearly appears.

According to Ferrari,[1] the predominance of the left hand is most seen under ergographic experiments. Ferrari's female cases are of the most use as regards the work done by the right hand, and with the dynamometer, they exhibit greater strength on that side. But with the *ergograph* it is just the opposite : the flexors of the left hand possess very considerable powers of endurance, much greater, comparatively, than is the case with men.

The ergogram given by the left hand is not only greater than that furnished by the right, but the woman has no sensation of fatigue with the left ; women can, at command, retrace a new curve with their left hands, possessing the characteristics of the curve made by the right hand.

Now, let us compare the *sexual signs of strength* and of *powers of resistance* in the two sexes.

As regards the sexual signs of strength, measured by the dynamometer, (the general comparison between a woman's and a man's strength), it is, according to our calculations, 570-1,000, that is, a difference of 43%.

[1] Ferrari, *Ricerche ergografiche nella douna*, Rivista sperimentale di Freniatria, XXIV 1898.

As to the sexual signs of the powers of resistance, measured by the ergograph (the general
comparison between a woman's powers of
endurance in work, and those of a man), it is
639-1,000, that is a difference of 36%, according
to Schouteden's experiments.

The result of these experiments is, that the
ergographic power is proportionally more developed
amongst women than amongst men. Amongst
women, their powers of endurance when at work
give them the strength for momentary effort;
but woman is more able to produce a
sustained moderate effort than to make a great
momentary effort.

These experimental conclusions agree with
Mosso's statements. The size of a muscle is a
distinct thing from its capacity to furnish a large
amount of work over a long period; it will
enable a man to raise a heavier weight, but it will
not enable him to lift a moderate weight a greater
number of times. The different results which
are observable amongst women and amongst
men, between the two methods of the quantitative
reckoning of mucular strength, therefore, furnish
us with a means of appreciating the *qualitative*
difference which exists between the two sexes
from the point of view of strength : as oft
repeated moderate effort suits the woman better

than a maximum effort made all at once. This idea, which may be applied to industrial labour, acquires quite a peculiar interest at the present time, when women's labour has become so much more general. We see the necessity of a most careful *selection* of working women with regard to their muscular powers, for individual differences are very clearly marked.

Ever since 1899, we have insisted on the absence of a complete correlation between the dynamo-metric test and the ergographic test, even from the point of view of the individual.

This idea is in perfect accord with other observations which clearly establish the fact that the woman has greater powers of endurance than the man, even from the absolute point of view. Hence the quotient of mortality amongst women is less than that amongst men, except during certain periods of life ; 16 women of 103 years of age may be reckoned against one man of the same age.

At all ages there are more women than men, although more boys than girls are born. At the end of the first year, of 100,000 born alive of both sexes, the difference in favour of the female sex is 2,677, and this difference attains its maximum, 6,739, at the age of 67 years. Certain Insurances which grant pensions, increase the annual pre-mium payable by women by 50%. There is an

excess in masculine births and an excess in feminine life.

Other proofs of this are supplied by the very
causes which determine sex.

Amongst these causes there is one, the importance of which is sufficiently well proved.
It is recognised in the animal world, as well as
in the human, that the determination of sex is
made under the influence of nutritive conditions,
and that good conditions favour the production of
the feminine type. The statistics collected by
René Worms [1] in France, are very significant in
this respect. He studied, not only the cases of
children born alive, but also of still-born children ;
these latter had never been included in statistics,
which led to the latter being incorrect.

The theory of nutrition enables us to take into
account the feebleness of the male as well as the
excess of masculine births. Nutrition being
dependent on economic conditions, the connecting link between biological and social phenomena was seized. According to Worms, the
progress of wealth and general well-being reduces
both the birth-rate and the number of male births.
The poor departments of France (Lozère, Mor-
bihan) shew an equality in grown-up males.   In

[1] R. Worms, *La sexualité dans les naissances françaises.*
Vol. de 237 p, Paris 1912, Giard and Brière.

Paris the excess of males falls to the minimum when the parents are of the same age, whilst it rises again when the disparity of age between husband and wife is greater. It is higher amongst working men than amongst employers. It went up slightly after the war of 1870. To these returns, we will add that the figures we have had occasion to collect during the present world-war, shew a larger excess of male births than is usual.

Well before Worms, Niceforo, the Italian,[1] seems, in his book on the *poorer classes*, which was published in 1905, to partly maintain the same thesis. William J. Thomas (1897) also considered that the poor populations shewed a larger proportion of male births than the wealthy. Raseri proved that in years of famine and of war, more boys than girls were born.

Worms' statistics are, nevertheless, the most complete, and justify the construction of the nutrition theory on solid grounds. How are these facts to be explained which seem to be opposed to the ordinary belief that the man has, as a rule, greater strength than the woman? If the woman, says Worms, is born with more abundant alimentary reserves, that would facili-

[1] A. Niceforo, *Les Classes pauvres. Recherches anthropologiques et sociales.* Vol. de 244 p. Paris 1905 Giard and Brière.

tate her existence, but it would restrain her from an activity which might increase her powers and her social productiveness. Selection is more severe for man and, at the same time, more useful to him.

De Greef (Brussels), struck by these results, has gone as far as to say, that the sex which is pretended to be the weaker, is really the stronger, it has the greater powers of resistance to the forces which destroy life ; it is also the more difficult to produce ; it requires the most advantageous conditions. Zoologists consider that the female is the strong sex, and that the male is the beautiful one.

Let us examine this opinion and put ourselves the question of finding out if the female sex can really be called " strong."

The answer must be supplied by physiology, and not by sociology, or even zoology. A greater " vitality " is not the equivalent of strength. And besides, the word " vitality " is not well chosen ; we are dealing with longevity, with " viability," as it were. Strength and longevity might even be opposed to one another: Let us consult anthropometric results.

The figures given below represent the female quantities expressed in masculine hundredths.

Height and weight of the body 88·5 to 94 (from 100).

Weight of the brain, 90 (Broca is different).

Weight of skeleton (femur), 62·5.

CO_2 exhaled in 24 hours 64·5 (day labourer), (Andral and Gavarret 1843).

Vital Capacity (18 years), 72·6 (Pagliani, 1876).[1]

Force of pressure on dynamometer (hands) 57·1 (labourer, Ioteyko).

Force of traction on dynamometer (bringing the muscles of the back in play) 52·6 (Quételet, 1869).

Test of power of resistance to fatigue (ergograph) 63 (Schouteden).

This table shews that, in a general way, the woman is to the man, from the physical point of view, as 80 to 100, which is what Manouarier also affirms, but the co-efficients are very unequal according to the information given. The result is the lowest where it relates to momentary effort measured by the dynamometer (57% and even 52%) : the strength of the man is almost double that of the woman. This last test is characteristic of strength ; it necessitates a sharp, sudden effort, an energetic and rapid discharge of nervous energy. This is an attribute of the masculine sex.

[1] By Testing respiratory organs by the spirometer.

The facts will appear still more significant when we examine the development of dynamometric force in connection with the age of children. Girls are weaker than boys at all ages, but the difference is slight up to the age of 11 years, and it increases steadily after that age. The difference in the curves for boys and girls, become more and more accentuated as they approach the age of puberty. Furthermore, the girls' strength ceases to increase to any extent in certain curves, after the age of 14 years.

And if we compare the development of muscular strength with those of other anthropometric aptitudes, we discover other differences that are no less characteristic. The difference in weight and in stature between the adult man and woman, is about 10% in favour of the man. But at one given point of growth (towards the period of puberty), girls are superior to boys in this respect. This superiority lasts three years for the stature, and seven years for weight. Now, preponderating strength is never for a moment in their lives, shewn by girls ; Consequently, *even when the weight and height of girls is greater than that of boys, their muscular strength does not, in consequence, suffer any increase.* Muscular strength is, therefore, in certain respects independent of general growth. It is in the highest degree a characteristic of sex. It is at the period of puberty that the difference in muscular strength is accentuated and definitely established.

Anthropologists, when studying the difference between the sexes must, therefore, not forget this striking fact : in the law of physiological differences, *muscular force* (momentary effort), constitutes a specific characteristic of the masculine sex. To this, one might add the *difference in the elevation of the voice.* Men of small stature are muscularly stronger than even tall women, and they have deeper voices. The difference in strength is partly because men have larger masses of muscles, and partly to peculiar qualities of their motor system.

But the woman has, comparatively, more power of resistance. In certain cases this greater power of endurance is absolute, as in resistance to sickness, in her longevity, in the determining cause of sex. In other cases, it is relative, as in the ergographic test. The co-efficient is, in this case, equal to 63%, whereas in the dynamometer it is 57%.

Now, the metabolic (changing) conditions (of nutrition), are quite different in the case of strength, and in the case of " endurance." The exhibition of strength demands a sharp,

violent expenditure of energy, and is followed
consecutively by exhaustion, during which
strength is renewed and nutrition obtained.
Thus the action is intermittent, only a limited
quantity of nutritious matter being parted with
on condition that it is rapidly replaced. These
two conditions, the power of acting instan-
taneously under a stimulating impulse, and the
ability to rapidly replace the losses suffered,
are the characteristics of strength.

It is quite different with the power of endurance.
That requires a slow and gradual expenditure of
energy, accompanied by little fatigue, or even
immunity from it. Neither must we lose sight of
the fact, that resistance may also be purely
passive, even in muscular work (inertia of the
bones and articulations). The work of endurance
is incontestably more economical, more productive, and less exhausting than the expenditure of
spontaneous force. Each of these forms of energy
has its uses, and its necessities, each represents a
distinct function.

It follows that we may again accept an old
physiological idea which pretended that man is
above all a " katabolic " being (breaking down),
that woman is an " anabolic " being (building up).
This anabolism, peculiar to woman, is surely
directly connected with the maternal functions

allotted to her. In creating lives, woman does not transform energy, she bestows it in its nutritive and chemical form.

Man personifies strength, the woman is the expression of endurance. This resisting power in woman should dispel many accepted prejudices, which have represented her as " eternally wounded," and needing care every hour of her life. Now, except under certain conditions, it is only in pathological cases that this is true. Under the usual physiological conditions, woman is vigorous, full of resistance, and robust ; and during this European war, has not the work done by women in every sphere of life (including work in munition factories), and in every belligerent country, given one more proof of the enormous amount of energy and power of endurance of which that sex is capable, which has been called " weak " by superficial observers, who are now recognised as having been mistaken.

The physical inferiority of women from the point of view of " strength," properly so called, which is proved by her having a much less well developed muscular system than that of man, is, we believe, congenital, nevertheless that inferiority has been considerably increased by want of exercise, in following the law of least resistance. The original cause (of a biological kind), has created a certain predisposition, a dislike common to most young girls, with regard to physical exercises. This repugnance should be overcome, because, on account of the law of the least resistance having come into play, it has passed physiological limits. It might become morbid if a suitable physical education did not correct this predisposition to a sedentary life, and thus lead to all those evil results to health that might follow in its wake.

2.—A NEW THEORY OF RIGHT-HANDEDNESS.
THE PSYCHO-PHYSIOLOGICAL THEORY.

We cannot, within the compass of this book, deal with all the different theories that have been advanced in explanation of the origin of right and left-handedness.[1] One thing seems certain, and that is, that asymmetry is congenital, but that it has been considerably increased by the almost exclusive use of the right hand.

Amongst recent theories may be mentioned that which has been put forward by Herber.[2]

[1] See : J. Ioteyko, *Théorie psycho-physiologique de la droiterie.* Revue philosophique, June and July, 1916.

[2] J. Herber ; *Essai d'une théorie clinique de la droiterie.* Memorandum laid before the *Académie de Medecine* 12 Nov. 1912.

This doctor, convinced that the only cause of right-handedness was a clinical one, asserted, as the result of prolonged and extensive observations, that the sufferings, movements, and efforts of the left side of the body react so powerfully on the heart that it is only natural, in following the law of least resistance, that man should have almost exclusively developed the use of his right hand.

The agonising attacks in the chest (angina pectoris) during which the pain in the heart so constantly reaches to the left arm, might lead to the belief that there are connections between the two organs undiscovered by dissection. Other observations have established the effect of lesions of the left arm on the heart. Potain and his pupil Lasegue, have described a series of experiments in which lesions of the left arm caused palpitations, or anginal troubles or hypertrophy of the heart.

Neuralgia in the veins of the left arm, or the amputation of the left arm, may bring cardiac maladies in their train. According to Ollier, Huchard, and other clinical surgeons, experiments clearly shew that the lesions of the whole of the left side of the body may react on the heart. Amongst invalids, rather violent move-ments of the left arm cause cardiac attacks.

H

There are probably anatomical connections which, unknown as yet, will explain these clinical symptoms, and shew the action of the heart upon the whole of the left side of the body.

This hypothesis, as to the origin of right-handedness, published by Dr. Herber in 1912, had been recognised by us as early as 1907, and, so as to test it, we started some experiments which we did not make known until 1916. Our point of departure was the following. Right-handedness is certainly not acquired by individuals, it is a phenomenon common to man, and has existed from all time, though in a less degree. Hence, there must be some important cause to account for its origin. The various theories and hypotheses advanced by different writers are not satisfying, even though they very likely contain some part of the truth. Now, when speaking of right-handedness, or left-handedness, it is first of all necessary to keep " strength " in view, as a distinctive characteristic ; skill is a differentiation of evolution, whilst strength is primitive.

Now, amongst the effects of muscular labour, that which it exercises on the heart, is certainly the most important to the organism as a whole. The heart-beats are quickened, and that to a very considerable extent.   The over-strain of the heart is often brought about by too much physical work.[1]

In physical exercises, the first thing that it is necessary to avoid is over-taxing the heart. And, moreover, death from fatigue, which does occasionally occur, in very exceptional cases (the classical example is that of the runner of Marathon), is due to the stopping of the heart. That organ first of all precipitates its beats and ends by becoming exhausted.

Heart fatigue is, therefore, the rock to be avoided when taking muscular exercise in the widest sense, and an excess of exercise is exacted, when a man no longer has only his own weight to bear, but also performs supplementary mechanical work in displacing heavy weights.

It would seem natural therefore, to admit *a priori*, that some mechanical automatic regulator must exist in man, some protective mechanism to act in conjunction with the heart, whereby the consequences of too great a strain are avoided. And we have thought that this protective element might very likely be found in right-handedness, by inciting man to *by preference* use, in the performance of heavy work, either the right hand only, or both hands together,

[1] *See* our article *Fatigue* in Ch. Richet's *Dictionnaire de Physiologie*, Alcan.

but always saving the left hand from working by itself, which, by its situation in the neighbourhood of the heart, seems likely to be in closer touch with that organ than the right hand.

We have submitted our theory to experiment. We advance it, not as a clinical theory, but as a *psycho-physiological theory of right-handedness*, seeing that we attribute to it a biological and psychical significance.

These experiments were begun in 1907, in collaboration with Mlle V. Kipiani, and were continued during several winters, in the psychophysiological laboratory of the Brussels University, on some of the students there—male and female. Herber quotes a certain number of pathological cases which support our opinion and which completes it on the clinical side. But his opinion, in spite of that, remains purely theoretical. That is why we think it may be well to make our experiments known, as they furnish an experimental contribution to the problem. We will now describe our experiments. We admit then, theoretically, that the same muscular work achieved by the left hand should be more harmful to the heart than that identical work when done by the right hand. As a criterion of cardiac fatigue one may examine the *acceleration of cardiac beats*, resulting from the work of each hand.

The experiments were made on 32 people, students of our course of psychology in the psycho-physiological laboratory in the Brussels University (22 male students, 10 female), of about 20 years of age. The work required of each arm was the following : the fore-arm being bent on the arm, a weight of 2 kg. and a half was given the student to hold in his hand. And, following the rhythm of a metronome, the student (standing in upright position), had to raise this weight above his head until the upper arm was extended to the full, every two seconds. The men were required to raise the arm 30 times, the women 20.

The general trend of the experiment was this. The students were assembled in a neighbouring room and each one came into the laboratory alone. Once there, they were required to keep absolutely quiet for several minutes. One knows, as a matter of fact, that it is enough to take just a few steps for the pulse to become distinctly quicker. After this rest, the rapidity of the radial pulse per minute was taken (by means of simple palpation) and the number of pulsations was written down as the normal state. After which, the student executed the movements described, with one hand. The number of pulsations was then immediately noted. The student then left the laboratory and waited in the adjoining room, leaving the field clear for other experiments. He returned at the end of at least half an hour and the same experiment was then made upon him on the opposite side. In the third place the effect on the heart of performing the work with both hands simultaneously was studied, each hand holding 2½ kilograms.

In other experiments the dynamometric strength of all the students was measured so as to separate the right from the left-handed, or, more accurately, to discover which were stronger on one side than on the other. All these experiments were made on different occasions upon each person, and in spite of a co-efficient error, inevitable in experiments of this kind, they gave very clear results. The task required was a very tiring one, (judging from those on whom it was tried, and also by noticing their attitudes), the respiration was halting, and the complexion flushed.

GENERAL TABLE.

*Acceleration of the radial pulse under the influence
of Muscular Exertion.*

(32 subjects).

GROUPS	Work with the right arm quickens pulse per minute.	Work with left arm quickens pulse per minute.	Simultaneous work with both arms quickens pulse per minute.
	Pulsations	Pulsations	Pulsations
Left-handed men	5·1	6·5	10·7
Right-handed men	6·4	7·1	7·2
Left-handed women	4·0	9·2	9·0
Right-handed women	4·0	7·2	9·0
Averages ..	4·87	7·5	8·97

We will first consider the general conclusions
to be drawn from this table and we will next
examine the differences, by groups.

The general averages (taken by including the
men and women together—the right and the left-
handed) shew that *exhausting work when accomplished by the left hand, produces a more intense
(more injurious) effect on the heart, than the same
work when performed by the right hand ; the*

difference is equal to about one third. In causing both hands to work together and consequently by causing a double effort in the same space of time, the cardiac acceleration is not the total of the two accelerations together but it is less by one quarter.

In passing on to the groups we obtain more precise results.

Amongst *right-handed men,* the effect on the heart is almost identical in the case of work with either hand, as well as when both hands work together. The advantage of bi-manual work is clearly shewn.

Amongst right-handed women, the results differ, in that the work done by the left hand exhausts the heart almost twice as much as the work done by the right hand. Bi-manual work is an advantage, but less than is the case with a right-handed man. The advantage amounts to one fifth.

Amongst *left-handed men,* work done by the left hand is more tiring to the heart than work done by the right hand. The difference equals one fifth. The simultaneous work of both hands tires the heart rather less than the total of work performed by each hand separately. The difference equals one tenth.

Amongst left-handed women, the work done by the left hand tires the heart almost two and one half times as much as the same work done by the right hand. The simultaneous work of both hands tires the heart to the same extent as that done by the left hand.

We can now interpret these results and draw some conclusions from them.

The fatigue of the heart, which appears to be much greater among women, who work with their left hands, than amongst men, may be attributed to two causes. The test was certainly more exhausting for them than for the men. They, in fact, frequently complained of it. In the second place, we attribute to the woman greater cardiac excitability than to men. When questioned on this point, several of our female students stated that they not infrequently experienced palpitations.

Amongst the left-handed, men as well as women, the work done with the left hand is more injurious to the heart than that done by the right hand, but the difference is less marked in the case of the man (left-handed), it is very marked in the case of the woman (left-handed).

One can therefore, say, that two essential conditions make work with the left hand particularly injurious to the heart : on the one hand, left-handedness (predominance of strength on the left side), and, on the other, the feminine sex.

*As regards the simultaneous work of both hands,
this presents considerable advantages, for right-
handed and for left-handed people as well, both for
men as for women.*

We see the idea which served as our point of
departure clearly confirmed—we know that work
performed with the left hand must produce a
more injurious effect on the heart than the same
work performed with the right hand.

And it is with a certain degree of probability
that we recognise that the original cause of
right-handedness is due to defensive mechanism,
intended to protect the heart against the effects of
the great strain caused by the excessive use of
the left hand. The results of these experiments
shew also a very remarkable gradation which
cannot be due to chance.

It is clear that the degree of harmfulness due to
working with the left hand is not the same under
all circumstances. Various pedagogic and industrial conclusions flow from this. Observe
that the work exacted was of a kind to require,
from the subjects of it, as great an aptitude from
the point of view of strength as from the point
of view of powers of endurance. In this the
woman is clearly shewn to be the inferior. From
this it follows that the danger to be avoided for
them in the exercises used in physical education,

as well as in industrial work, is the performance of work which puts too great a strain on the heart. Careful supervision should be exercised in this respect, even in normal cases.

In cases of cardiac disease, the woman should be dismissed from certain kinds of hard work. But do not let us forget that work with the right hand or bi-manual work may often be allowed.

As regards the greater fatigue shewn by the left-handed, working with the left hand, to the right-handed, working under the like conditions, the explanation is still surrounded with great obscurity. But it seems very probable that the left-handed person, who is strongest on the left side, is naturally inclined to develop a larger total of work on that side. The result of this is, a warning to left-handed people (those who in preference if not exclusively use their left hand), to avoid certain heavy employments, such as unloading of goods, removing of furniture, etc., at least unless they have, through suitable training, become ambidextrous.

The clear result of these experiments is, that it is more dangerous for a person to be very markedly left-handed than right-handed. Left-handedness appears, to the present writer, to be a defective adaptation, it is necessary to correct it. The left hand, therefore, in the case

of a left-handed person, should not be developed
from the point of view of strength, because then
it will be used to excess, and will produce great
fatigue of the heart. In developing their right
hand, and placing it, as far as possible, on an
equality with the left, ambidextrous conditions of
work will be created, and those are the most
advantageous of all. In no cases, however, will it
be possible to change the left-handed into right-
handed people, seeing that, with them, the right
hand hemisphere is more developed, and con-
genitaly more perfect than the left hand hemisphere. The left-handed persons will thus remain
left-handed for the more complicated kinds of
work, works of skill, such as do not require great
muscular effort.

In conclusion then, it is the over-work of the
left hand that should be avoided, and that more
in the case of the left than the right handed,
more in the case of women than of men, more in
the case of people with excitable hearts, and
above all, in the case of those suffering from
heart disease.[1] Amongst right-handed men, the
harmlessness of working with the left hand only
is only apparent ; as a matter of fact we have

[1] If the left-handed people were completely inverted, that is
to say, if their hearts were on the right side of their bodies,
it would be working with their right hands that would be
harmful to them. But the inversion of the viscera is extremely rare.

only had to do with remarkably robust individuals; injurious effects might have made themselves felt after more arduous work.

The teacher, even whilst respecting natural tendencies, should institute exercises amongst his right-handed pupils too, especially amongst those markedly right-handed, for the correction of what is excessive, and to allow of the child's making use of both hands.

Why not praise *bi-manual* education (a term which we prefer to ambidexterity), when we see its excellent results in those experiments where the work was accomplished by both hands simultaneously ? The result does not seem insignificant when we compare the figures given by Orchanski, who says that, at the present time, 25% of the trades require the simultaneous development of both hands. This necessity for the use of both hands, we may add, is very clearly apparent in the occupation of a soldier ; we may be allowed to say that an ambidextrous education, if begun in childhood, should certainly have most unexpected results in that relation.

Our theories of right-handedness go beyond the limits of pure physiology ; we have, moreover, called them *psycho-physiological*. It is, as a matter of fact, very probable, that the right hand has developed greater strength on account of the reasons given.   It is a superiority acquired during man's phylogenetic development.   This supremacy carries others in its train. The work of the right hand has reacted on the left hemisphere, and has produced its supremacy, and that not only from the psycho-motor standpoint, but also from the point of view of sensitiveness, skill, and intelligence, because of the connections existing between the different centres. The difference between the two hemispheres, at first physiological, has, in the course of time, become psychological.

In fact, it has been proved that asymmetry not only bears on the centres of perception, it also affects the centres of speech, of recognition (the loss of which produces amnesia, or the impossibility of recognising objects or signs), and the powers of co-ordination (the loss of which constitutes ataxia or the impossibility of executing the proper movements for arriving at a given place.   We will not penetrate into the region of the centres of association.   Now, these centres, among right-handed people, are localized on the left side.

We believe that it is due to the operation of the law of least resistance, that the left hand has been condemned to inaction, and the right hand has acquired an exaggerated development.   This

one-sided localization of a great many of the
centres of perception, and of the centres of association, seems to us to be acquired and is certainly not free from danger to the healthy
integrity of cerebral action. It has passed its
functional destiny by a long way.

3.—AMBIDEXTROUS EDUCATION.

The practical conclusion come to in the preceding chapter is as follows : *Ambidextrous education has for its aim, the correction of the excessive
supremacy of one hand over the other, a supremacy
which far surpasses original asymmetry, because
of the almost exclusive use of that side of the
body that is best endowed, and by virtue of the
law of least resistance.*

This necessity for correction being admitted,
the degree should be decided on. Now, the
law of least resistance has been so effective,
that the training for the work of all the industries
of civilisation is based on the activities of one
hand only, and one cerebral hemisphere only.
The increased growth of asymmetry is proved by
means of the dynamometer (p. 97).

We have elsewhere refuted Félix Regnault's [1]

[1] F. Regnault, *Pourquoi on est droitier ?* Revue scientifique
13 June, 1914.

objections, for he considers asymmetry to be a
sign of superiority because it is almost unknown
amongst animals, very slightly developed amongst
savages and very marked in civilized man, less
marked amongst women than amongst men,
amongst children than amongst adults. This
is to believe that our civilization has brought
us nothing but progress. Alas! this is the
reverse of the truth! Nothing illustrates this
better than the tables relating to myopia, which
show that this affection, almost non-existent
amongst the peasantry and the uncultured,
increases strangely in proportion to the degree of
education, up to the point of being most accentuated amongst university men. Yet no one
would consider myopia as a sign of superiority.
It is an annoying consequence—but avoidable—
of a certain state of things. It is the same with
asymmetry. That a pathological foundation
would sometimes seem necessary for the bursting
forth of genius we will not deny, and a strong
portion of asymmetry may perhaps, in that respect, be an advantage. But we have never seen
pedagogy strive for deformity in order to attain to
an object as obscure as it is uncertain. One cannot
consent to the extinction of the most feeble organ.

We commend ambidextrous exercises quite as
much because they are healthy for the practical

centres as because of their practical utility. We mean, not only gymnastic exercises, but also games, manual work, drawing and writing.

In England, it was John Jackson, founder of the *London Society for Ambidextrous Education*, who became the promoter of bi-manual education. The results were excellent. In Germany, we have the name of Pabst (Leipzig) ; in Belgium, Sleeys and Tensi, Mme Michiels, ourselves, and our pupil, Mlle V. Kipiani. In the United States bi-manual education is current in the schools.

The wisdom of carrying this bi-manual education as far as the training of the left hand to write, has been proved by Fraenkel's clinical observations. This doctor has reported cases of invalids whose right hand being paralysed, also suffered from aphasia. Upon their learning to write with their left hand, they began to develop the right centre of language and thus regained the power of speech. This shews the close connection between speech and writing, and the enormous part played by writing in the development of cerebral functions. The energy gained by bi-manual education is valued by Fraenkel at 50%. The students, the labourers, artisans, soldiers, are all visibly benefited. Writer's cramp will no longer exist, since the hand will no longer suffer from over-work.

I

These facts shew the wisdom of training the left hand to write and to draw. The use of speech is one of the most intellectual powers of man, and drawing is also connected with one of our highest functions (art),

The hand, which is the servant of the brain and one of the chief instruments for the execution of the wishes of that organ, should be developed bi-laterally. It will thus become possible to develop those treasures of the mind which have lain hidden in the dormant cerebral hemisphere condemned to certain death for the want of cultivation. According to Orchanski, the harmonious development of both sides of the body may exercise a very considerable influence upon general development, and amongst backward children who shew difficulties of speech, it may help the acquirement of language. Certain statements seem to contradict this opinion. Thus, Ballard has pointed out the frequency of stammering amongst left-handed abnormal children, who are taught to write with their right hand. But we must not forget that in the left hemisphere, in the case of left-handed people, neither Broca nor Wernicke's centre is developed, both being developed in the right-hand hemisphere. It is clear that, if writing can be accomplished by one hand, it will be done by the better hand, which, in the case of a left-handed person, would be the left hand. By quite reprehensible inconsequence, people try to transform the left into a right-handed person, and only train one side (the right hand one), whose action on the centres they wish to develop is nil at the commencement of the effort.

Under these conditions, according to Stier's opinion, trouble may arise, owing to a struggle for supremacy between the two hemispheres.

4.—ALIMENTATION AND WORK.

In the course of studying the different conditions of labour,[1] we have, in collaboration with Mlle V. Kipiani,[2] examined 43 Brussels vegetarians, all healthy, who had not adopted this unusual regimen for therapeutic reasons, but for moral or hygienic reasons. All were total abstainers, and only used coffee, tea and chocolate very sparingly. These people belonged to the intellectual class of workers. We examined their dynamometric strength, their powers of resistance to fatigue were tested by the ergograph, their vital capacity by means of the spirometer,

[1] J. Ioteyko, *Les lois de l'ergographie*, Bul, de l'Acad. Roy. de Belgique, classe des Sciences, 1904, extract of 174 p.

[2] J. Ioteyko and V. Kipiani, *Enquête scientifique sur les végétariens de Bruxelles.* Pamphlet ot 77 p. Brussels, 1907.

and the rapidity of their nervous reaction by means of d'Arsonval's chronometer. The comparison of the mechanical work accomplished by the vegetarians, and that accomplished by the omnivorous, is very significant. We see how enormously the vegetarians are benefited. The omnivorous people, however, with whom they were compared, were rather powerful University students, whilst the vegetarians were in no case of herculean appearance. In the average, one might estimate the increase of mechanical work, due to a vegetarian diet, at 50%, if we omit one single ergogram, which was carried to the limit of fatigue.

The *form* of the curves gave results no less interesting. This increase in the mechanical labour of the vegetarians was not made at the expense of the heights of isolated contractions; on the contrary, the contractions in their cases were a little shorter than those of the omnivorous It is their *number* which is considerably increased. Their number is often doubled, nay, even tripled, amongst the vegetarians, when compared to the omnivorous. *Vegetarians can work for two or three times as long as the omnivorous can, without becoming exhausted.* This effort is distributed with greater regularity, amongst vegetarians ; their curve keeps at one level for a long time and is very slow in its descent. The curve of the non-vegetarians is higher at the beginning, but the descent is rapid. It gives the impression of there being, amongst the latter, a dissipation of their strength at the beginning of their work, and that their effort cannot be long sustained.

From the point of view of productivity, it is much more profitable to extend labour over a long period, even though it be a little less energetic, than to expend a greater amount of energy in a short period only.

A third point shews the incontestable superiority of vegetarians. The recovery from fatigue is much more rapid amongst them than amongst the omnivorous : *two minutes' rest between the curves, suffice for the recovery of the whole of their powers amongst vegetarians.* Under the conditions of the ordinary regimen, ten minutes, at least, are required.

As regards the calculation of strength by the dynamometer, the averages furnished by the vegetarians are almost identically the same as those supplied by the omnivorous. No loss of strength can be proved here. For the purpose of comparison we will use the experiments already quoted for both the dynamometer and the ergograph.[1] The vital capacity was measured by

[1] See the experiments by Schoutenden and by myself.

means of Verdin's spirometer. The vegetarians shewed a vital capacity superior to that of the non-vegetarians (volume of air expired after forced inspiration).

The time taken for nervous reaction (in acoustic excitation), is no longer among vegetarians than among non-vegetarians. This is of great importance from the standpoint of industrial accidents (see p. 39).

We are, therefore, justified in saying that a vegetarian working man would not be more subject to industrial accidents than an omnivorous workman. But, as vegetarians tire themselves less than the non-vegetarians, they are really less liable to those accidents incidental to their work.

Such are the principal conclusions which result from this impartial enquiry, of which the sole purpose was, to gather scientific information bearing on powers of work under various experimental conditions. They are entirely in favour of a vegetarian diet. The progress of alimentary chemistry, and of physiology, has super-abundantly shewn that an entirely vegetable diet is compatible with the preservation of health and strength. On the other hand, they have disclosed the dangers of a carnivorous diet, the producer of auto-toxines. Auto-toxines are the sources of various maladies (belonging to the cycle of arthritism) and they exercise a paralysing action on the muscles. On the other hand, we know that in order to keep the human body in good condition, some albuminoids are required and in order to produce energy, a good supply of carbohydrates is necessary. These latter are found more abundantly in the vegetable than in the animal kingdom. Bouchard has rightly said : that a meat diet is not conducive to the performance of muscular work. Neither is there anything to shew the necessity or the utility of a meat diet, for brain work. Only, the transition from a meat to a vegetable diet is painful in some cases, and strong and tenacious prejudices are opposed to the general adoption of a vegetarian diet.

We may conclude that, *in tests of their powers of resistance to fatigue, vegetarians are proved to be superior to non-vegetarians, whilst in tests of strength and in tests of speed they are equal to them.*

These proofs have an economic and a social bearing. Hygienists and sociologists should not turn the working man away from a vegetarian diet, which is the most economical, and at the same time the most productive from the stand-point of work, and may also be looked upon as one of the best means of combating

alcoholism.[1] Unhappily, the idea still generally obtaining to-day, is, that meat alone is
strengthening.

We had the honour of seeing our book on
the study of vegetarians, approved by the
Academy of Medicine. Now, to-day, when the
necessities of war have made it absolutely necessary
to lessen the consumption of meat, we have heard
Dr. Maurel, at the same learned assembly, make
a speech (in January, 1917), shewing that France
requires from 900 millions to a billion kilograms
of proteids per annum, to feed her, that is a daily
consumption of from 75-90 grammes of albumen
per adult inhabitant. Now, this amount, said
Dr. Maurel, is largely provided for her by the
vegetables she grows—notably by cereals, dry
vegetables, potatoes, etc. Furthermore, milk
adds about 240 million kilograms of nitrogen
to this. As to the meat consumed, even in the
towns which use the most, they scarcely supply
from 25-30 grammes of nitrogen per adult—
that is—a third of the necessary quantity.
Moreover, the proteids of either fresh or frozen
meat are three or four times as expensive as
those provided by vegetables, and, after a certain

---

[1] Vegetarians are quite naturally abstainers, because they
are not thirsty.   Vegetable foods contain the necessary amount
of water, and neither do they awaken thirst artificially, which
is the case with meat.

limit is passed, constitute less healthy food than the latter. For these various reasons, *there is no cause for alarm*, concluded Dr. Maurel, *if our supply of meat leaves something to be desired, since our vegetables can supply us more cheaply, and in a more healthy form*, with the full quantity of proteids of which we are in need.

And when France decided, at the end of the third year of the war, to prohibit the use of meat for two days a week, she, at the same time ministered to an economic necessity and a hygienic need.[1]

5.—USE OF THE LEFT HAND BY THE WOUNDED AND MUTILATED.

(Some Scientific Rules for Re-education).

The problem of re-educating those wounded in the war,[2] revives certain anthropological and physiological neuro-muscular questions, which are receiving a new kind of application in connection with a new and interesting class of people, and the necessity suddenly arises for

[1] See : J. Ioteyko and V. Kipiani, *Le Végétarisme et son influence sur la santé publique, le Commerce, l'Industrie et l'Économie de la nature.* Report of the International Food Congress, Ghent, 1908. Pamphlet of 68 p.

[2] J. Ioteyko *L'usage de la main gauche chez les mutilés. Quelques regles scientifiques de rééducation.* Revue Scientifique, No. 16, 2nd sem. 1916.

establishing this re-education on solid scientific foundations, with the object of restoring to our wounded,—if not the normal use of their injured limbs,—at least a shadow of that use, and above all of permitting the substitution of one limb for another, and the apprenticeship to a new trade. This idea of re-education is not entirely new ; for a long time now, those crippled by accidents in the course of their work, have been cared for and re-educated in Schools *ad hoc*, with a view to restoring them to society, and preserving them from beggary, the thousands who,—victims of our economic system and its dangers,—each year pay their contribution to an industrialisation pushed to an extreme.

But that which is very exceptional, even in the most, industrial countries, has become very common during the war ; those who escape death return crippled, lame, deaf, paralysed. And one sympathises with all the attempts made to build up these maimed, imperfect, amputated bodies, so as to make them capable of again taking their place amongst the active in this world,—amongst the workers able to gain their daily bread.

Those mutilated in the war must be numbered by the thousand, if we are to take all the belligerents into account.

How many there are who have lost an arm! The loss of one of the upper limbs is very unequal in its effects on the sufferer, according to whether it is the right or the left arm that is lost. As most people are right-handed, the loss of the right arm is much the more serious, and the re-education of those crippled in battle is complicated by necessitating the education of the left arm, which has remained, so to speak, inactive up to now. And it is with this education of the left arm that we are going to deal in this section, in the hope that these pages may be of some use to those who have the task—the heavy and grave responsibility of re-making, of restoring those mutilated in the war, of just those who, having to live by manual work, find themselves suddenly deprived of their productive organ, their one and only possession,—of one arm, if not of both ! Dr. Fraenkel, already quoted above, has reported cases of wounded, paralysed in the right hand, who, at the same time suffer from aphasia. In teaching them to write with their left hand, they also develop the right centre of language. The paralytic thus recovers the power of speech. One single experience of this kind is of greater interest than the whole of a vain argument. It demonstrates the direct connection between speech and writing, and the enormous importance of writing in cerebral functions. These facts clearly explain the theory of aphasia, formulated by Broca and which led to the discovery of the centres of articulate language. Now, the centre of speech is located in a convolution situated in the posterior part of the lower frontal convolution in the neighbourhood of the centre of writing. The exercise of the left hand cannot, therefore, be confined to gymnastic movements only, but, just as speech is one of the msot intellectual functions of man, so also is writing and drawing, because the latter, although manual acts, nevertheless touch one of our highest functions (ethics and art).

From these premises we draw the following practical conclusions ; *it is indispensable, in the treatment of those suffering from aphasia, due to the loss of an arm in the war to make them learn to write and to draw with the left hand, so as to develop a new centre of speech which will be situated in the right cerebral hemisphere.*

We have many times boasted of other advantages attaching to ambidexterity,—the cure of writer's cramp which is common amongst those employed in clerical work, the better utilization of strength in the various manual employments, and, finally, the immense advantage it gives those who, in cases of paralysis or amputation, are in a position to use the arm that remains intact. Certain it is, that late training can never attain an equal proficiency to that acquired at an early age. If ambidexterity had been a common practice, those now mutilated in the war would be much more capable of acquiring the required skill with the left arm, having been originally trained by games, gymnastics, drawing, writing, manual work, and even by certain arts and handicrafts.

The training of the left hand amongst those maimed in the war, has now become an inevitable necessity and we can only rejoice to see that previous experiments in ambidexterity are so much in favour of such training. It goes without saying, that the left-handed man who is maimed, must, in like manner develop the right arm, but it remains to be shewn under what conditions such training should be carried out. This is what we will now enquire into.

To begin with, one remark must be made. We cannot here speak of "Ambidextrous," or "bi-manual" education, as we generally do. Those on whom the experiments are to be made, have had one arm amputated, and it is a question of how to give the remaining arm the strength and skill necessary to the acquirement of some handicraft.

This training of the left hand should be directed by several principles. It is highly advantageous to enable the man to keep to his original occupation, —that is to say—*to teach the left hand to execute the same movements as those which had been executed by the right hand.* This principle has been very clearly established in the attempts to re-educate the maimed, as it has been recognised in practice, that the experience gained by one hand is an advantage to the other.

How is this remarkable fact to be explained? It has been experimentally demonstrated, notably in some of our researches,[1] that the work performed by one arm reacts on the other, either by increasing its excitability, or by diminishing it, as the case may be.

This evidence proves that the state in which the psycho-motor centres of one side exist, is more or less reproduced on the opposide side. Other observations demonstrate that the same is the case with acquired movements. If you ask a person to write with the left hand, you will notice that after several futile attempts, he will succeed, without much trouble, in tracing presentable letters. And, the curious thing is, that the writing of the left hand will bear the

[1] *J. Ioteyko,* L'effort nerveux et la fatigue. Archives de Biologie XVI, 1899.

impress of all the peculiarities of the writing by the right hand,—it will reflect the personal characteristic element which enables us to recognise each person by his hand-writing.[1] These statements which were handed to us to verify, after the experiments made by Mlle V. Kipiani,[2] a pupil in our laboratory, shew several points which are of real value,—in the first place, that the movements acquired by the left hemisphere (which directs the movements of the right hand), are transmitted to the right hemisphere, and, secondly, that this transmission is not purely and simply an increase of excitability, but that it comprises all the complicated movements necessitated by the act of writing, in a word, that the characteristics of handwriting certainly have their origin in some central cerebral cause.

According to Dr. Meige, the graphic education of the right hand is reflected as in a *mirror* on the upper left limb, and, in a general way, the training of the motor centres of one limb has its corresponding effect on the symmetrical motor centres of the opposite limb. The effect of this training, though often latent, is none the less real and shews itself, when called upon, in the facility with which the untrained limb will reproduce the movements of the trained limb.

[1] This is most of all apparent if the writing is viewed in mirror.
[2] *See :* V. Kipiani, *Ambidextrie*, 103 p. F. Alcan, 1912.

These rules have already been applied in the treatment of convulsions and cramp (Meige) ; they are going to help us to establish the basis for the re-education of the maimed.

Consequent upon the opposing symmetry of the two halves of the brain " mirror writing " is looked upon as the normal physiological writing of the left hand. " Reflected Movements " is the name given to those executed by the left hand in contradistinction to those executed by the right hand. These movements are those which come the most natural to it,—the easiest of execution. From the moment when the right hand has adopted a system of working which seems to it the easiest, the left hand ought to make the same gestures whilst maintaining an opposite direction. It seems certain that a great number of failures in the training of the left hand, have arisen from exacting from it movements superimposed upon those of the right hand, and which are generally contrary to its aptitudes. It certainly cannot be denied that even identical movements exacted from the left-hand do produce satisfactory results in its training, but the true method is to educate the left hand by " reflection."

From these considerations we evolve the following rule : *Apprenticeship, with the left hand, to a craft, should be accomplished by following the law of the opposite direction ;* that is to say, that the left hand must not simply copy the right hand, but that it must execute all the movements of the right hand, but reversed. This should be the general rule, in the case of training to a new trade, as well as in the education of the left hand for the same craft which was formerly followed with the right hand.

And in returning to the examples quoted above, regarding those suffering from aphasia, we say, that it would benefit them to exercise them in writing with the left hand " by reflection " (as well as in drawing " by reflection "), with the object of developing as promptly as possible, the centre of writing on the opposite side, and by its instrumentality acting on the centres of speech on the right side (motor and sensorial centres).

We will consider one last question. Can the left hand be trained to any and all handicrafts without reserve equally well ? The limitations we are going to make are based upon the results of our own experiments.

The general results are as follows :—*heavy work with the left hand produces a more considerable effect on the heart than does the same work when accomplished with the right hand ;* the difference is about equal to one third (4·87 accelerations per minute for work by the right hand, and 7·5

K

accelerations per minute for that by the left). By working both hands together and thereby furnishing a double amount of work, the cardiac acceleration is not the total of that observed when each hand works separately (4·87 and 7·5 =12·37), but it is less by a quarter (8·97 accelerations). It is, therefore, better for the heart that the work should be performed by both hands simultaneously than by each hand separately. This result pleads strongly for ambidextrous work, and it shews the harmful effects upon the heart of heavy work performed by one hand alone, and that the left.

With regard to the conclusions to be drawn from these experiments from the standpoint of the re-education of those crippled in the war, we would say that *the use of the left hand alone* (*in the case of the loss of the right arm*), *cannot be applied to all industries* in view of the harmful effects of heavy work by the left hand, on the heart. It is here that a group of our subjects of experiment, did now shew any difference between work done by the right, and work done by the left hand, but since the others shewed an enormous difference to the disadvantage of the left, the first group, would, without doubt, have betrayed a like difference if tested by heavier work ; and although the experiment was not made, it is only reasonable to conclude that this is so.

It is impossible for us to specify the industries that are unsuitable for the left arm working alone, it is for the medical specialists and for the teachers to decide each case on its merits, and they should be careful to examine the patient's heart from the standpoint of disease and of neuroses, which is the only possible criterion. In certain cases it would be better to change the patient's employment than to cause him to do that which is too exacting for his left hand. On the other hand, all crafts do not demand a large amount of expenditure of strength, and may be performed by the maimed who have only preserved the use of their left hands.

6.—LEFT-HANDED WRITING BY THE MAIMED.

For the right-handed wounded to learn to write with their left hand is a problem the importance of which is notorious at the present time. It is not only the necessity of giving the left hand some power of writing adequate to the needs of current life, a very few attempts would suffice for that. The question is a more complex one than that. It is requisite to give to the left hand exactly the same efficiency as the right hand possessed, making it possible for the wounded man to undertake various employments, especially that of a teacher, or clerk in an office, obliged to write with the requisite rapidity in ledgers, etc. A thorough training is therefore necessary, and lessons must be given with the co-operation of a competent teacher and a very practical method of teaching. By practical method we understand one that will satisfy the *desiderata* enumerated, and which, far from being inspired with theoretical questions concerning the reform of handwriting, is only bent upon attaining the desired end, it is, therefore, necessary to teach the left hand to write exactly in the same way as the right hand, so that suppleness may be absolutely assured. Preliminary exercise in " reflected " writing may, nevertheless, be of undeniable value.

Necessities created by the war, have caused processes of writing intended for the use of the left hand, to be evolved. We particularly recommend the two processes—identical in their main lines—commended by two professional men who understand the problem, and who take a personal interest in it ; both having been deprived of the use of their right hands, long before the war began, they have themselves been obliged to face all the difficulties inherent in the task of writing with the left hand in order to prosecute their callings (of an office clerk in the first case, a schoolmaster in the second).

According to M. Meurville,[1] the failures in the training are due to defective attitudes : the copy-book was placed upright, very much to the left of the body, the arm remaining glued to the chest, the wrist turned backwards. The writing was upright, uneven, and produced with difficulty because of the contraction of the muscles of the arm, the wrist, and the fingers. The fatigue which resulted was discouraging. This writer considers that it is as easy to write with the left hand as with the right, and therefore, to accomplish all the clerical work usually performed by the right hand. The same advice should be given for writing with the left hand, as for writing with the right hand, that is, free movement. Only the position of the copy-book must be quite different. In order to secure from the left hand a perfect English hand writing, differing in no particular from 'hat of the right hand, the following directions should be followed :—

The copy-book should be placed in front of the pupil, not quite in the centre of the chest, slightly to the left, and sloping towards the right.

---

[1] Meurville, *How to write with the left hand*, Nos. 4, 5, and 6, 1916. *Journal des Mutilés.*

The chest should be upright and leant lightly on the right arm [1] of which the fore-arm is resting on the table, the hand resting on the copy-book. The right side of the body should be about 5-6 centimetres from the table. The left side, about 10-12 centimetres off. The left arm should be separated from the chest by about 20-25 centimetres. The fore-arm should have the same slant as the copy-book, and the elbow will act as a pivot which will move towards the chest, as and when the pupil writes. This movement will allow of the left hand writing on a surface of from 6-7 centimetres. The pen chosen should be fairly soft and should not be held stiffly.

The most practical and most rapid type of handwriting is flowing English. A great effort should be made to form each word without raising the pen with the hand,—the movement of the fingers only should come into play in the formation of the letters, the work of the hand and of the fore-arm being to move the fingers from one end to the other, of each line, beginning on the left. The movement of the wrist will only be needed

[1] This statement, of course, applies only in the case of training persons possessed of both arms to write with the left hand, as well as with the right. In the case of one-armed men, the right stump (if any), might be used to steady the book, if the stump is long enough, or fitted with an artificial limb.—*Ed.*

when the large loops of the capital letters have to be formed.

To get the slope of English writing, it will be advisable to exercise the fingers in sloping towards the right, a movement easily acquired in the course of a few days. The copy-books or writing copies in use in schools for right-handed pupils can be used for left-handed beginners.

With the left hand, one can write an upright hand equally well. Round-hand and medium writing (in which the slant is mid-way between that of English and upright writing), can also be accomplished.

According to M. Albert Charleux lessons in writing with the left hand should be taken at very short intervals. The first attempts are scarcely ever encouraging and the pupil is doubtful of success. Another stumbling block to avoid is that of wishing to get along too quickly.

The first attempts should be made with chalk upon a blackboard (or on black paper fixed against a wall). At first, the arm should be held at full length, then, gradually the drawing should be reduced until at last, it only needs a movement of the wrist. These exercises (small drawings the models of which will be found in the text) should be executed standing upright, without stirring the feet, and without bending the body.

The hand, the arm, and the wrist having thus obtained a preliminary training, the pupil will complete his education by applying himself to the drawing of letters on the blackboard. The size of the writing should vary from 15 mm. to 2 centimetres. It is not until after these stages that writing in a copy-book should begin.

With the right hand, the copy-book is slightly inclined towards the left ; with the left hand it should be slightly inclined towards the right. For either hand the elbow forms a pivot about which, the fore-arm moves in the same direction namely from left to right. The left fore-arm, which is what we are interested in at the present moment, describes a line which tends towards the body as it descends towards the right. The penholder should be lightly held, and it is necessary to raise the pen as seldom as possible. The paper will be held steady by means of a paper-weight. When the maimed are able to write a flowing hand, they may learn to write round-hand.

This similarity of the two processes, which in reality only constitute one, is an argument in their favour. The only difference is the preliminary exercises in M. Charleux's method, which, according to M. Meurville, are useless. However, this may be, children who shew a certain difficulty in learning to write, get on well when they first trace words on the blackboard. It may be rightly said, that the adult pupil is not in exactly the same position, having already practised writing with the right hand, and we know that a training acquired by one psycho-motor centre transmits itself to the opposite side. The adult would, therefore, have fewer difficulties to conquer were it not that with age the manual adaptability diminishes as a rule. We, therefore, think that preliminary exercises may not be altogether useless, although not indispensable, they may help to graduate the difficulties, and consequently to shorten the period of apprenticeship, and to make the steady progress made by the pupil more evident.

At the moment of going to press with this book, another study on the art of writing has appeared, by a M. F. Garcin.[1] In order to acquire the English handwriting and the medium handwriting, with the left hand, the copy-book should be placed upright in front of the chest, so that the travel of the left arm will always be in prolongation of the line of the slope. In short, M. Garcin says, when writing with the left hand, the line of the slope should always be in the

[1] F. Garcin, *Comment écrire des deux mains.* Paris, Nathan, 35 P.

direction of the axis of the left arm.   As regards writing with the right hand the line of the slope should always be perpendicular to the chest. We must remember that the line of the writing is the straight horizontal line upon which the writing is traced, whilst the line of the slope is the position of the axis of each letter in relation to the line of writing.   The position of the body always remains the same.   The result to be obtained from the left hand should be exactly the same as that given by the right hand, but the two hands act by executing directly opposite movements.

We will now give an account of the interesting experiments made by the Polish military doctor, Adolphi Klesk, who having had to deal with a number of those injured in the right hand, warmly advocated left-handed writing. According to his observations, an adult man learns to write with his left hand after three or four weeks' training This study is beneficial for those who have had arms amputated in the war, for it not only enables them to write, but it also acts in an encouraging way on the patient, by giving him a proof, as it were, that the left hand if properly trained is capable of learning some kind of craft.   It is with writing then, that a beginning should be made, for to learn to write with the left hand constitutes a powerful pedagogic, medical, and social asset. To begin with, the left hand has a tendency to execute " reflected writing," and it is by an effort of will of about eight day's duration, that the ordinary handwriting gains the upper hand. To begin with, too, the left hand becomes very easily tired. The rhythmic movements of the fore-arm slipping along the paper without detaching the edge of the palm of the hand from the copy-book, are very difficult to acquire. The author recommends the writing of letters on a large scale on a blackboard during the time of training, and, when writing in a copy-book, the use of soft, glazed paper and soft pens and pencils.

Encouraged by the results of his experiments, Dr. Klesk recommends ambidextrous writing to parents, who should, at an early age, teach their children to write with either hand, which amongst other advantages, would result in a more symmetrical development, and assure the use of the second hand in the event of an accident or illness. He especially cites the malady known as " writer's cramp," which is met more often amongst office clerks than amongst literary men, because the former have to preserve the aesthetic side of handwriting ; this trouble may become so chronic that the sufferer finds himself obliged to change his occupation.

These observations of a military doctor are now of such practical interest that we have thought it interesting to recount them here, although they in reality, only confirm the results of our early experiments.

IV.

BELGIAN METHODS OF TECHNICAL EDUCATION.

I.—PROGRESSIVE TECHNICAL EDUCATION THROUGHOUT BELGIAN SCHOOLS.·

The close collaboration of science and industry will, in the near future be pressing, and numerous are the tentative experiments already being made, both in England and in France, with the object of finding the most adequate solution to the agonising problem of after-war necessities. In order to study it properly, it is necessary to begin at the beginning, at the point where technical instruction begins ; that is to say, even in the primary schools, which are supposed to give to the citizens of the future a general education, and to follow it up in the secondary schools, and in the professional, technical, and industrial colleges.

We will make a tour of this kind, through the Belgian schools, keeping the communal and provincial schools principally in view.[1]

[1] J. Ioteyko, *Les Méthodes belges d'éducation technique.* Revue générale des Sciences, 30 May, 1917.

Manual work, from year to year, acquires increased importance, in the schools of the town of Brussels.[1] " Very soon now," says A. Nyns, Inspector of Primary Education, " Manual work will form the basis of all our teaching, because of its intuitive, concrete, practical, and experimental character."

Henceforth, the child will learn as much through the hand and the tool as through the brain and the book.

The first courses of manual work were opened at No. 12, Primary School for Boys, at Brussels, in 1879.[2] The subjects taken were joinery, wood-turning, modelling, and locksmith's work The classes were held for from four to five hours every day, and the pupils were expected to pass through each workshop. The teaching of manual work had, at that period, a triple object ; (1) the manual education of the child ; (2) the industrial education of the children of the working classes, to prepare them, in a general way, for taking up various trades ; (3) to cultivate a taste for handicrafts by popular classes.

In 1883, M. Sluys, Director of the Brussel's Manual School for Teachers, and M. Van Kalken, a professor at that school, undertook a journey

[1] A. Nyns, Les travaux manuels a l'Ecole primaire. Pamphlet of 24 p., Brussels 1910.
[2] Needlework in Girls' Schools is of much earlier date.

to Sweden, in order to study in that country a really pedagogic organisation of manual training It was in 1885, that there was opened in Brussels the first normal course for the instruction of teachers in woodwork, cardboard work, and modelling, following the general methods of the Swedish teacher Otto Salomon. In 1887, when the first batch of teachers were qualified to teach the manual work, this branch was entered on the curriculum of the *Normal Schools*, and of *all the Schools in the city of Brussels*. Manual training, said the town programme, is looked upon as a means towards the physical, intellectual and moral development and perfecting of children. We cannot aim at the direct teaching of special trades. What is aimed at is, to develop general ability, quickness, dexterity of both hands, prompt and firm movement, a taste for and a love of work, and to inculcate habits of order and correctness, to develop the faculties of attention and perception, to supply a more complete and a deeper intuition of geometric ideas and forms of calculation and the metric system, and to make the pupils more persevering by application to work, to shew the necessity of producing nothing but complete and correct work, to cultivate the sense of beauty through the harmony of form and colour of the objects made, and to inform the pupils with a knowledge of the technical processes which constitute the foundations of scientific industries.

The methodology of manual work for boys requires the analysis and understanding of models and of tools, the demonstration of the process of execution, and the construction of model types. The pupils are gradually exercised in the handling of tools.

The curriculum for the first standard (children of from 7-8 years of age) includes : folding, cutting-out, joining, weaving, and modelling.

The curriculum for the second standard (children of from 9-10 years of age) includes : the art of making cardboard articles, modelling geometrical solids from plaster casts, common objects from nature, from memory, and of their own invention, etc.

The curriculum for the higher standard (children of from 11-12 years of age), modelling and wood-carving. The pupil's work from models or plans. The models first copied are horizontal or vertical projections, or *sections*. The aesthetic side is most carefully attended to. The course of wood-carving is given in a workshop. The programme provides for ten and a half hours per week, for the six years in a primary school, one and a half hours for each of the first three classes, and two hours for each of the three upper classes.

Although the teaching of handicrafts in the primary school is of a purely pedagogic kind, it is none the less true, that thanks to the training of the hand, and of the eye, which it involves, this work develops the qualities of skill, indispensable in the acquisition of a manual trade, whatever it may be, which must influence the ultimate special training of the pupils.

We will not here discuss the handicrafts in the secondary schools. It will suffice to mention their existence in all these schools and the existence of several well equipped workshops, bright, light, and spacious, newly built, near secondary schools, rejoicing in every modern appliance and comfort, as, for example, Léon Lepage's secondary school at Brussels.

The children leave the primary school at 12 or 13 years of age. A few continue their studies in the secondary schools or in the athenaeums ; the large majority are the children of the people, and wish to devote themselves to some handicraft after leaving the primary school. But they are still too young to at once enter the training colleges and also too weak from the physical standpoint.

The *Secondary Schools* (or Upper Primary Schools), are intended to give these children a

L

supplementary general education to enable them to master such knowledge as may prove most useful to them in life, whilst waiting until they are old enough to enter a technical school. The course of study in the Fourth Standard Schools lasts two years. The Fourth Primary Standard education includes three distinct courses,[1] (1) the Fourth Standard for girls ; (2) the Fourth Standard for boys of professional and commercial tastes ; (3) the Fourth Standard for boys desiring an industrial career. The Fourth Standard for girls is intended to complete the general education of the pupils, and to initiate them in one of the businesses connected with needlework. They are, in short, popular small training schools where the apprenticeship is served amidst scholarly and moral surroundings. The course consists of the study of two languages (French and Flemish), of arithmetic, commerce, natural sciences, technology, hygiene, social economy, domestic economy, the history of civilization in Belgium, commercial geography, music, gymnastics, and swimming.

The Fourth Standard for boys with professional and commercial leanings, prepares youths for administrative and commercial occupations ;

[1] A. Nyns, Les ecoles de 4 degré, pamphlet of 14 p. Brussels 1910.

those with tastes for handicrafts it trains for manual work.

We will consider the latter. The children are not apprenticed to a trade, but are taught the modus operandi of the various callings. Furthermore, the scientific and theoretical knowledge imparted to the pupils will be of great service to them in their manual work. Manual work can be usefully applied to other branches of the curriculum such as designing, calculation, geometry, physics, social economy. The pupils do modelling and cardboard work, they do wood and iron work. The courses of study have an essentially practical tendency, and are given with a view to their application to trade.

The curriculum of the city of Brussels, says, in substance, that the object of these schools " is to assist in the formation of a working class which possesses an intelligent knowledge of the work it performs, which is master of the machines it employs, which reads and thinks, and which is conscious of its, own dignity." After this general and technical preparation, the pupil, now about 15 years of age, can freely enter any technical school to serve his apprenticeship to the calling he has chosen.

Amongst the *Fourth Standard* schools, that of *Saint-Gilles* (Fauburg de Bruxelles), called the

Morichar School, counts as one of the most important in the country. Its Head Master, M. Devogel,[1] has won for it a peculiar distinction, and has made it a model school which has never yet been surpassed. It will be interesting, we think, to give a detailed description of this school, basing our account on official documents, and on the memory of many personal visits.

The Upper Primary School should not, says M. Devogel,[2] be a duplicate of the Secondary School. It is absolutely necessary to create an organization for the working class, whereby their sons can receive a general education preparing them for all callings, to establish a school where the children of the people, and of small employers, who do not wish to adopt administrative work or become employees or clerks, can receive clearly specialised manual training,— to found an institution where, in a word, the son of the working man, who *wishes to remain a working man*, desirous of starting on what we call a *manual career*, can, whilst developing himself as a whole, at the same time prepare himself for his future social function.

The most useful knowledge to the working man

[1] At the present time Director of the Brussels schools.

[2] V. Devogel, *L'Ecole primaire supérieure technique de Saint-Gilles-les-Brux lles* (called 4th Standard), pamphlet of 104 pp., Brussels, 1911.

includes *Mathematics*, the *Sciences, Design,* and the *Handicrafts.* To these must be added the two national languages (French and Flemish), history, geography, industrial economy, some knowledge of accountancy, hygiene and technology. Design includes industrial design, and ornamental design. Handicrafts include forestry, agriculture, masonry and metal work. They are completed by a course on tools which is the synthesis of the whole. Technology is completed by numerous visits to studios, workshops, and factories, paid during the scholastic year and during the journeys at the end of the year (five days). Lantern lectures are used for a great number of the courses; geography, technology, etc. The scholastic year winds up with an exhibition of all the work of all the pupils. All courses are compulsory.

Let us examine the *method* adopted in the teaching at the upper primary school of Saint Gilles, which prides itself on being only a primary school. Its special characteristic is the inter-connection of its different branches, the constant connection of the different courses, and the intimate union between the lessons. Thus, the different branches of mathematics are constantly intermixed and combined with industrial design, ornamental design is combined with modelling, with wood-carving, metal work, etc.

The school has stoutly declined to practise methods based upon abstractions, holding that that can only be an end, which is the logical outcome of a whole series of anterior, concrete, material sensations. A certain formula has lately, says M. Devogel, achieved a great success in our country : *the school for life.* It is either ingenuous or incomplete. It says either too little, or says it badly. It is simply *Life in the School* that should have been written, and that is the motto of Saint Gilles.

" A school should reject," the Belgian teacher goes on to say, " all that is not living, thus conforming to the evolution of existence, to the life of man, to social science, to the science discovered by humanity. Life in the School. Let us be inspired by that, and let us open wide the doors and the windows of our classes."

Every branch of instruction is looked at from this point of view. The elements of design are found in geometry and in nature ; these two sources should be explored in succession. Geometry leads to the discovery of the meaning of a line. The line being known, the vegetable or animal element will be drawn quite naturally. All designs are based on drawings from nature alone ; copying is not allowed. Designs have to be made with the most diverse materials as medium, the pen, black and coloured crayons, red chalk, charcoal, chalk, brush-wash, water-colour, water colour and gum, oil colour, pastel. Plaster models have been suppressed, when necessary a natural model being given to each pupil (plant, shell, insect). Perspective is taught from the landscape (the drawing of a door, a wall, the staircase of a hall, of a country cottage). The child is allowed to colour his drawing as often as possible.

The most important branch of the education given is handicrafts, based upon geometry and design—both in close relation to them. The school of Saint Gilles aims at giving the pupil a manual training as wide as possible. " Yes," M. Devogel says, "let him acquire his manual humanities." Give to the artisan of the future the sense of economic life. One might easily fall into specialisation here ; now, it is not our object to specialise. Aesthetic development should also be striven for. Good taste is of essential importance to the artisan. To attain this end, it is indispensable that the child should be made to *work in as many raw materials as possible and with as many tools as possible.* Consequently, the school was established like a *laboratory for handicrafts.*

The school does not wish to act as a substitute for the workshop. It is here that *talent may be awakened.* And, M. Devogel adds, when compulsory education up to the age of 14 has become law,[1] the Fourth Standard School will become the natural sequel to the primary school for the children of the people.

Let us take, as an example, iron work. The first thing made is a plate, out of sheet-iron for the handle of a drawer. Each pupil has a model. This is analysed by the class and the teacher, as to its nature, its object, its utility, its raw material, its shape, and its dimensions. The pupil takes the exact measurements, and makes a free-hand sketch. They then adjourn to the workshop. The teacher gives the necessary technical explanations with regard to the tools, the work, etc. Each pupil makes the object according to the pattern. Nothing is more curious than the *lesson of invention.* The pupils are asked how the type of the plate made out of sheet-iron may be altered eventually. The pupils try to find out, and give their answers.[2] Finally, how is the plate to be ornamented? And what shall the ornamentation be? What tools shall be used, what machines, what moulding, what lines? The pupils then go home and think, and are thus taught to use their own initiative or

[1] Compulsory education in Belgium became law shortly afterwards.
[2] Devogel, *loc. cit.*

enterprise, and to exercise their faculty of invention. They all, always succeed in producing good results. This lesson, by which the pupils acquire a method, is adapted to the capacities of the scholar. He searches, he discovers, he invents with his own faculties. The pupil's imagination is kept awake, developed, and excited. By the end of the year, articles are made *in unison.* The whole class then forms only one workshop and the pupils discuss the outlines of the project, the details to be made, etc. It is a true initiation into social life, and the happy results of this process will accompany the future workman during the whole of his career.

We can estimate the value of the teaching at the Fourth Standard School of Saint Gilles, by glancing at M. Mattot's two manuals, he being a teacher at the school. The first of these manuals is devoted to a *Course on tools and handicrafts,*[1] the second,[2] to *Metal work in the Student's workshop.* In the preface of the first of these books M. Devogel asks for *compulsory education up to* 18 *years; primary, upper primary, and industrial.*

[1] A. P. Mattot, *Cours d'outils et de métiers manuels.* Vol. 328 p. with 354 engravings, 1912 Brussels. Preface by M. V. Devogel. Lebègue.

[2] The Same : *Le travail des Métaux a l'atelier scolaire* Vol. of 214 p. with 128 engravings, 1913 Brussels. Preface by M. V. Devogel, Lebègue.

The Industrial School, under the *University of Labour*, would comprise the continuation of primary, and upper primary studies, and the handling of tools of a mechanical type. Apprenticeship, in other words specialisation, would be served or taught in the workshop, the timberyard, the factory. Everywhere, from 6 to 18 years of age, teaching should have general development and the awakening of vocational talent, as its aim ; everywhere the dream would be *to form the man.* These will be the " humanities " for manual or technical craftsmen.

General technology will play a considerable part in this programme. The workman of the future will thus be liberally instructed. The *technical education* of man will thus be realised. Through all the stages of education it will stand side by side, and rank equally with physical, intellectual, moral and aesthetic education. It will be studied at the same time as these other subjects in the primary school. In the upper primary school, and in the industrial college, it will be based on a solid foundation of mathematics, natural science, and design. The course on tools is more than synthetic, it is adopting M. Paul Hyman's saying the *philosophy of Manual work.*

M. Mattot, quoting Franklin, says, " that

which distinguishes man from the other animals is, that he manufactures tools." The author gives very complete lists of tools, he distinguishes 20 classes of them. Each instrument is described, and a very precise idea is given of it. The book is illustrated with 350 engravings.

The second book is devoted to *metal work*. It is a complete guide to raw materials, to tools, and the procedure of working in metals, with suggestions for exercises for the first (13-14 years of age), and second (14-15 years of age) years' training.

We see that the school of Saint Gilles fully accepts the *pedagogic theory of handicrafts*, which the Americans have formulated in the following manner.[1] " The scientific theory of education through the handicrafts is definitely established. All conscious movement has its origin in an excitation of the motor cells of the brain. Thought without action, may develop the imagination, but leaves the will-power uncultivated. Will can only be developed through action. All muscular movements react on the brain cells by sensation, and fix themselves in the centres of association in the form of perceptions and images. In order to increase the receptivity of the brain, a rational education requires that we shall vary

[1] O. Buyse, *Méthodes américaines d'éducation générale et technique*, 3rd. ed., 1913, Dunod and Pinat, Paris.

the nature of the movements exacted by manual work, so that all the other groups may be interested in succession. From these facts it is evident that, in order to develop the entire motor region of the brain, full and various exercises must be multiplied, and directed in such a way as to sharpen the sensitiveness, to quicken thought, and to strengthen the will. If the movement becomes a habit the result of this will also be that it will be made without reflection and will cease to develop the motor cells, and, therefore, cease to have any educational value. It is only during the first period of excitation, that the action of manual work is efficacious. Exercises pushed beyond the educative point, may become the means of preparing for more advanced work, of an industrial kind, but they can no longer be ranked amongst those which contribute to general development.

" The result of this is, that the educational action of the various forms of manual work should be measured by the progression of the mental reactions which they are capable of provoking. This is why some teachers cause girls to perform the same work as boys, in the primary, and even in the secondary schools."

In a recent article,[1] M. R. Astier, a senator

[1] R. Astier, *Les travaux Manuels*, Le Journal, 15 May, 1917.

and president of the Commission on Technical Education in France, asks why the question concerning the reorganisation of industrial education in France, officially propounded in 1905, has not yet been answered. One reason for this regrettable inertia is due to a prejudice, far too wide-spread in France, which has a tendency to look down upon manual work as derogatory. Now, M. Astier affirms that there is no thorough technical teaching without manual work. That constitutes its base, its point of departure. Now, owing to a national fault which has become more pronounced during the last century, the Frenchman seems to look upon manual work as " servile work." He will not see that without it the most ingenious creations of the mind, the ideas of a Papin, a Pasteur, of a Berthelot, could not have been realised. The one ambition of the middle classes for their sons is that they should enter either the liberal professions or become officials.

We believe the danger to be even greater than M. Astier warns us of, because the working classes themselves think they are raising themselves a step in the social scale by pushing their sons into bureaucratic careers. We have seen what Belgium has done for the workman who wishes to remain a working man. It seems as though it might be possible to efficaciously oppose these bad tendencies and prejudices by a suitable education. There are various ways of presenting work under an agreeable aspect. In the first place, the feeling of human solidarity makes one happy and proud to contribute to a common task, not with the object of enriching the master, but for the common good of society. Therefore, all that exalts and ennobles labour should be made clear. In the second place, there is the aesthetic side. For this the works of poets, sculptors, and painters who have made the apotheosis of labour should be popularized. Force, courage, perseverance, all have beauty. And the clank of metals, the heat of factories, the flames of the furnace, coal mining, all speak an appealing language, more proud and attractive than that of the peaceful occupations of a bureaucrat.

Now let us pass on to *technical education* properly so-called ([1],[2],[3]).

Councils for the improvement of technical teaching have been formed in Hainaut, in Brabant,

[1] J. Ioteyko. *l'Université du travail de Charleroi et le probleme de l'apprentisage* (Revue générale des sciences, 15 fevrier, 1917.

[2] Charles Gheude, *l'Enseignement technique dans le Brabant.* Publication de la Ligne de l'Enseignement, 21 p. Brussels, 1912.

[3] J. H. de Wemel, *Enseignement technique pour jeunes gens et adults.* Enseig. de la ville de Bruxelles. Broch. de 45 p., 1910 Brussels.

and in Brussels. The technical training of the workman has been placed in the first rank of the social problems of the day. The numerous technical schools founded by the city of Brussels have many aims, they are principally : to improve the craft, so as to train picked workmen (school of jewellery, of typography, book-binding, gilding, lead work, plumbing, mechanics, etc.) ; to put the young men of the country in a position to carry on, in their entirety, trades to a great extent monopolised by foreigners (school of hairdressing) ; to remedy the inadequate preparation in languages, and accountancy ; to fight against " machine-ism ; " to give birth to a taste for the beautiful and good ; to enable national industries to successfully sustain the struggle against foreign competition (school of lithography) ; to keep in touch with progress ; to improve public taste by improving the artisans ; to democratize teaching by making it accessible to all ; to create a remunerative trade ; to revive a trade, fallen into decay by reason of a difficult apprenticeship and rudimentary organisation ; to fight against an immoderate infatuation for office careers ; to prevent the artisan from becoming reduced to the rôle of a mere machine without any ideals ; to take physical and intellectual aptitudes into account ; to avoid the creation of inefficient artisans who would encumber the trade ; and to establish a connection between the various trades that have points of contact. The complementary teaching of ideas in which young people might be lacking, the study of all papers of technical interest, the forming of special libraries, holding lantern lectures, visits to museums, monuments, factories, excursions, the exhibition of works of past scholars, all combine in making up an exhaustive curriculum.

It is impossible to speak of each school separately. We must be content to indicate the methods of teaching adopted in some of them.

The characteristic of the teaching in the *School of design, modelling and wood-carving*, consists in (contrary to the special academies of design and modelling, which generally only teach from the classics) teaching the pupil how he should understand his work, the object of which is its application to the building and furniture-making industries. The subject given is first of all sketched, then modelled according to the sketch, and is finally executed in wood. The pupil is at the same time initiated in a knowledge of the different styles employed in decorative art and furnishing. At the technical school of *mechanics* the professors avoid empirical work and give the most rational scientific basis for the manufacture of the object to be produced. The construction of an apparatus is made in accordance with a plan sketched by the pupil, and afterwards verified by the master.

The teaching in the training school for *plumbing* aims at the training of certified sanitary plumbers, such as have been asked for by the various International Congresses of Hygiene. They furthermore endeavour to resuscitate the industry in ornamental lead-work. Sanitary technology is taught in two, three, or four years of study.

The pupil who leaves at the end of three years should be competent to, himself, elaborate a complete system of sanitary drainage and to carry it through in all its details. Drawing, physics, and chemistry are the subjects of serious study.

The industrial school of *ornamental tapestry* trains its pupils in the problems of aesthetics and art. An art decorator cannot ignore the distinctive characteristics of the different styles of house furniture, and inside decoration. A course on the history of art, answers this purpose the best.

The course for *typography* has for its object the training of picked workman in order that Belgian printing shall not only be able to compete satisfactorily with foreign productions, but also to recapture the prosperity and renown which she

M

enjoyed in Plantin's days. The creation of a style, of a national method, that will allow of the recognition of books printed in Belgium, just as this is the case with some that are printed in Germany, France, England, etc., each of these countries possessing a style of its own, is another object. The motto taken " raise the level of the typographic art," indicates a clearly artistic programme, which has a still higher aim,—*to make creative craftsmen*, without, however, neglecting the mechanical side, which becomes, more and more important every day. The courses in design develop good taste, the sense of observation, and the analysis of complicated subjects, and permit of the production of the complete work. The course on colouring has three principal objects : (1) To enable the workman to produce all the shades of colour with a sure hand, by a study of colour and material ; (2) To make of the typographist the direct collaborator of the artist by enabling him to acquire ideas on art, sufficient for this purpose ; (3) To enable the workman to use coloured inks. These three points are developed in thirty lessons in the theoretical course. The practical course consists of sixty lessons.

As far as the *book industry* is concerned, the city of Brussels possesses a *Technical* school *of*

Art-binding and gilding, where, side by side with subjects of a technical nature a course is given on the history of the book and of book-binding.

The *Commercial School* is a school for the training of clerks.

The city of Brussels has declared its determination to see the founding of *Normal Technical Schools*, and *Industrial Universities*, which shall constitute a *Federation of the Industrial Schools of the Kingdom*. A second resolve is to institute a propaganda in favour of *compulsory industrial training* as a consequence of *compulsory primary education*.

2.—THE CHARLEROI UNIVERSITY OF LABOUR.

The problem of Technical Education and training, ranks amongst the most important of our century wherein industrialisation is pushed to an extreme, and the problem has become exaggerated since events have rendered workmen scarce, even though, after war conditions should be marked by a renewed need, and an accelerated productivity. All eyes are turned, so to speak, towards that side of life, towards the best methods of organising it and fostering an increase of productivity.

We think that an enquiry concerning the Belgian technical institutions will furnish a really interesting study of activity, Belgium being the country where industrial production has attained to a rate unknown elsewhere in Europe at present, in proportion to the number of its inhabitants. The Charleroi *University of Labour*, which is well-known to the writer personally, thanks to visits and studies made upon the spot, has happily escaped the bombardment, from the effects of which the town itself has suffered terribly. For a description of it we will borrow the following passage from M. Omer Buyse, former director of the institution[1] " From the Mound of Waterloo which dominates the agglomeration of boroughs, of which Charleroi is the centre, the view stretches over a region which has not its equal in the world, from the standpoint of the concentration of industry and the density of the working-class population. In the foreground, the city which has not yet reached its full extent, and its suburbs, descends to the banks of the Sambre ; the industrial landscape stretches out beyond ; the framework of the winding gear of the coalmines is visible all over the place, and the landscape is punctuated with the rounded hillocks at the

[1] Omer Buyse, *Méthodes américaines d'Éducation générale et technique*, 3rd. ed., 1913. Paris 847 p. and 398 ills. The last chapter is devoted to the University of Labour.

pit-heads ; by the great bays of the glass works, the balls of cherry-coloured glass attached to the retorts of the blowers may be seen balancing themselves with a majestic rhythm. A multitude of chimneys belch out their black smoke ; the heavy outlines of the tall furnaces stand out against the foundries, forges, rolling-mills, work-shops for the manufacture of metal work, mechanical, and electrical, chemical factories, and those for refractory products. Of an evening above the steel-works jets of shimmering light rise up, which illuminate the foggy sky like a gigantic blaze of fireworks. Puffs of white vapour, escaping from the engines are the outward signs of the intense labour which the working population performs for its daily bread, at the price of effort and of danger, a thousand yards under-ground, and within the shade of the factories. The sight gives an impression of grandeur.

" The province of Hainaut could not have chosen a more appropriate site for the first University of Labour which it founded in accordance with the grand conception of M. Paul Pastur, its permanent deputy, and M. Alfred Langlois, at that time Inspector of Technical Education in Hainaut. That institution combines with the activities of that laborious region to dominate

the country like an ideal for the technical and
moral raising of the working class.

" The title, ' University of Labour,' which
covers the whole of the technical educational
system for Hainaut concentrated at Charleroi,
is very arresting to those interested in industrial
progress and the education of the working man.
A title of nobility, a tardy homage paid to
manual labour on which compliments and
favours are too rarely showered, because it is
performed by those whose education and training
has always been neglected ! "

The two buildings occupied by the University
of Labour cover a surface of three and three-
quarter acres ; the style of architecture is sober and
severe ; in the large hall stands the statue of
the Hammerer ' by Constantin Meunier. The
Institution was founded by the province of
Hainaut; the Belgian traditions of decentralisa-
tion, and communal and provincial autonomy,
give to communal and provincial administrations
the right of initiative This plan of action
permits of the existence of an organisation devoted to the local needs of the population. The
University of Labour has come into being in the
most industrial province in the country. Its
management was undertaken by M. Omer Buyse,
who had for a long time studied the conditions

of technical education in the United States of America. M. Omer Buyse resigned his post in 1914, only a few months before the outbreak of war, and the invasion of Belgium, for the benefit of the second University of Labour, which was to be founded in Brussels. The capital of Belgium did not wish to loiter behind on the road to industrial and technical progress, and it commissioned Mr. Buyse to organise a similar institution (which was also to include a section reserved for women), intended to act as a centre for the whole of the technical and industrial schools of the province of Brabant. What fate is in store for this new foundation ? We trust it awaits its realization in a not far distant future.

We will return briefly to the arrangement and the character of the various uses of the University of Labour at Charleroi, taking official documents as our guides.

The district of Charleroi includes six industrial communal schools, which have six thousand working children as scholars. In conjunction with these schools, the University of Labour has instituted a system of technical education, which comprises the *Industrial Day Schools* and *Industrial Evening and Sunday courses*, the middle stage being the *Upper Industrial School*, and the highest the *Upper Finishing Course*.

Thus, to every young man of intelligence and perseverance, this institution offers graduated series of courses that he may pass through (without being called upon to make any pecuniary sacrifices) and raise himself from the most modest social level to the highest point of technical knowledge.

One noteworthy characteristic of the method of teaching introduced in the University of Labour is the amount of experimental work done ; side by side with the theoretical course, a number of technical manipulations and experiments are made ; by this means a large amount of material is dealt with. It is thus that the physical and mechanical phenomena which form the base of almost all constructive industries are taught, in an experimental and quantitative form analogous to the conditions of the industry itself. For example, all the phenomena and the laws which refer to the flowing of fluids, are demonstrated by means of elaborate apparatus, such as a branch canal from the town water works, of which the pressure and supply are regulated by taps and measured by metres, and manometers. Ideas as to the mechanical properties of materials are verified on apparatus for testing by bending tension, compression, torsion and shock, identical to those actually employed in the industries themselves.   The courses on machine tools for joiners and modellers are supported by experiments on industrial machines ; ideas on boilers, steam kettles, etc., are taught by practical manipulations ; the course on electricity is experimental, as is also that on thermodynamics.

The *Eleven Industrial Evening and Sunday Schools* are intended for the training : (1) of printers and typographers ; (2) of plumbers and glaziers ; (3) zinc-workers ; (4) bakers ; (5) pastry-cooks ; (6) market-gardeners ; (7) locksmiths ; (8) tailors ; (9) industrial modellers ; (10) moulders and founders ; (11) electrical fitters. These schools only take young men who are really employed in the trade ; they are attended by 500 apprentices and workmen.

The bakery school of the University of Labour was the first to be established in France and in Belgium, and its establishment awakened keen curiosity in the bakers' union, the trade having been, in the highest degree, traditional. Amongst scientific trades, that which is taught in the plumbing school is of great interest ; it has preserved its manual character. As regards the school of electricity, the basis of the study, as here taught, is technical electricity which permits of experimental study in the electrical laboratory and in the generation of continuous and alternating currents, of the phenomena and laws of electricity, and of its application to lighting, its motor power and other transformations of electrical energy. The technological courses on electrical industries are nothing but one long succession of manipulations which are performed by the pupils themselves on some material connected with the industry, under the guidance of the teachers ; the theory of the operations is taught by a course of lectures delivered in the auditorium of the laboratory itself. Technical drawing plays one of the most important parts in this teaching. The evening schools have the effect of extending the scientific and trade knowledge of the workmen, and of widening their productive powers.

The *Industrial Day Schools*, are four in number, and have four school years : The School of Mechanics, the School of Electricity, the School of Joinery, and the Modelling School. They are attended by 700 apprentices, free of charge. The branches of trade taught here give the apprentices a preparatory training for every trade. In the first year's course, the beginners execute a graduated series of subjects in wood and in iron ; their aptitudes are indicated and their tastes are developed. At the end of the year they take up one technical speciality, which they choose under the advice of their teachers and parents. All the pupils do the work themselves, keep their own tools in order, and draw their own plans. The course on the technology of construction, combined with the mechanics and the strength of materials, completes the technical training of builders, etc. An experimental course on heat and steam engines completes the industrial training of mechanical engineers (automobile engineers, etc.). A wage of from 5-20 centimes per hour is paid to the pupils during their apprenticeship.

The *Upper Industrial School* is of a superior order. Those employers and workmen who have, thanks to their taste and skill, been able to leave elementary industrial schools and trade schools, have the means of perfecting themselves in the evening and Sunday courses of the *Upper Industrial School*, which are spread over three years because of there being only nine hour's attendance per week. In order to be admitted to the Upper Industrial School, the pupil must be 18 years of age, which assumes that apprenticeship must have been served, and the knowledge of a trade acquired. Six hundred pupils attended these courses in 1912-3 ; they were distributed among nine sections, which represented the large industries of the district, that is to say : (*a*) Mechanical Engineers and Draughtsmen ; (*b*) Electricians ;

(c) Civil Engineers ; (d) Mining ; (e) Chemical Industries ; (f) Metallurgical Industries ; (g) Industrial Arts; (h) Science of Accountancy; (i) Correspondents. And it is a most interesting sight to see the auditoriums and the laboratories crowded with men of from 18-20, sometimes 30 years of age, who, after the tiring occupations of the day, come there to attend courses for an additional three years. This effort is chiefly necessitated by the rapid changes in the processes of working. The Upper Industrial School takes an active part in the progress of this department of industry, by providing those workmen already trained with the foundations of a perfect scientific and technical education. The scientific character of the courses given here is clearly acknowledged. Besides, it is experience which is its essential foundation ; from the standpoint of experimental methods, the school possesses a wealth of appliances. In certain sections it is quite complete (the electrical for example). The metallurgical and chemical laboratories, with their spacious halls, are provided with tables to work at, with ovens and with all the apparatus necessary for the study of electrochemistry.

The *finishing courses in technology* are intended for all the young men of the wealthy classes destined to form a staff of specialists for the great national industries of the country. This course entails at least two hundred hours of instruction, and manipulation, and entitles the students to a *Technician's Diploma*. It now remains for us to speak of the *Technological Museum*. The first purpose of this Museum is to contribute to the improvement of the methods of technical teaching ; this purpose is attained by exhibiting the works of industrial schools, by normal courses, and by the central laboratory of the schools.

The normal courses for the Professors at the commercial and industrial schools, which have been given since 1905, are an indispensable complement to technical teaching. These courses are intended to attract those workmen and employees who have been selected by their Upper Industrial School for a professorial career ; these courses last for two years and are attended by 80 students.

The Museum sends, free of cost, to those schools which ask for them, its technological collections and its apparatus, to enable them to extend the field of their demonstrations, which are generally circumscribed ; these collections are also accessible to parties of scholars from other schools, when conducted by their professors ; industrial experiments and experi-

mental meetings are arranged for them in their
own laboratories, thus bringing those industrial
schools which are too isolated, into touch with
current ideas. Seventeen trade asssociations, of
which thirteen are under patronage, and four
artisan, aid its efforts to attract the industrial
classes towards a regeneration of labour.

The Museum possesses some superb collections,
such as apparatus illustrative of the types of
mechanism invented from the time of the invention
of the steam engine down to the present day,
collections connected with metallurgical industries, chemistry, ceramics, brewing, distilling,
and soap making, and which demonstrate synop-
tically the processes through which the raw
materials pass in these trades. The collections
in all their variety, serve to illustrate labour.
In the lecture hall of the library, visitors are
permitted to consult the books and to make
notes and plans.

A staff for commercial consultations exists
and gives most useful aid. We may also mention
intermittent courses for trained masters and men,
courses which make demonstrations and which
offer valuable help to those who think themselves
too old to attend the regular courses of a school
(they are attended by many thousands of
auditors), and systematically organised trade

competitions having for their object the stimula-
tion of the workman in his endeavours to attain
self-improvement. In this manner in the course
of a year, the University of Labour has organised
competitions between typographers, tailors, plumbers, masons, plasterers, and bakers.

To sum up the University of Labour, based
upon the principles of American methods of
technical education, brought over from the
United States by Omer Buyse, renders the greatest
service to the industrial province of Hainaut.
Opened in 1903 with 152 pupils it has collected
together a permanent population of nearly 2,000
scholars. The pupils trained in these schools
have materially contributed to the improvement
of the technical methods of factories and workshops.

3.—BELGIAN INITIATIVE IN THE INDUSTRIAL
RE-EDUCATION OF THOSE MAIMED IN THE WAR,
IN FRANCE.

In this triumph of applied science, the Province
of Hainaut has not forgotten the unfortunate
victims of accidents incurred in the prosecution
of their work ; it has dreamed of re-constructing

a new life for them, also based upon productive labour.

The *School for those crippled and broken by toil*, established by the Province at Charleroi, could certainly never have anticipated such a glorious destiny as was reserved for it only a few years after its foundation.   M. Herriot, Mayor of Lyons and Senator for the Rhone, has not hesitated to declare that " all the schools for the re-education of those wounded in the war must be regarded as branches of the *School for Cripples* at Charleroi."

Before recording the part played by Belgium, and particularly by the Province of Hainaut, in the work of the re-education of those wounded in France, let us devote a few words to the School at Charleroi.

Its inspirer was M. Pastur, permanent deputy for Hainant.   In the course of a minute enquiry he learnt that most of those maimed in the industries were condemned to idleness.   In collaboration with M. Caty, he, in 1907, laid before the provincial Council of Hainaut a paper entitled : *L'Assistance aux Estropiés par la création d'écoles d'apprentissage et d'ateliers.* (Assistance for the injured, by the establishment of schools of apprenticeship, and workshops). The authors asked that such a school should be founded for the Province of Hainaut, at Charleroi. The proposal was accepted, and that same year, a commission composed of MM. Pastur, Caty, Balthazar, and Dourlet, was sent on a mission to Sweden, Norway, Germany, and France, there to study industries for the maimed.

In 1908, the school for cripples was founded at Charleroi, the only one actually existing in Belgium itself,[1] and the first in Western Europe. The school was placed under the management of Dr. Dourlet.[2] The aim of the school is to place those injured in their work in a position to derive what benefit they can from whatever capacity for work there may be left to them ; for this a special training is required, based upon the nature of the physical handicap from which they are suffering, and upon an industry appropriate to their remaining powers. The *School for Cripples* is connected with the technical institutions founded by the Province of Hainaut, and to the Charleroi University of Labour in particular. Each apprentice, after the first month, receives wages, and meals in the canteen

[1] Several months before the war, the Province of Brabant took a similar step.

[2] Dourlet. *L'Ecole provinciale d'Apprentissage et les Atelier pour Estropiés de Charleroi*. Revue Psychologique, Vol. I 1908, pp. 280-287.

are free. The chief workshops are those for carpet - weaving, basket - making, brush - making, saddlery, harness-making, and orthopædics, and also schools for tailors, book-binding, and cardboard work, shoemaking and accountancy. The School for Cripples at Charleroi supplies a want ; the number of its pupils, from its first beginning, is the best proof of this. Its activities have rendered great services, by giving to the crippled, heretofore generally doomed to beggary and a life of privation, a craft which allows of their living honourably by their work. According to reports which we have received, the School at Charleroi has already begun to train some of those maimed in the war.

Several months before the war broke out, M. Herriot, the Mayor of Lyons, visited the School for Cripples at Charleroi. He was struck by its practical utility and its humane work. One saw, for example, a man who had had both fore-arms amputated, occupied, thanks to special apparatus, in nailing brushes ; one of the stumps bore a block of steel which served as a hammer, the other a leathern prosthesis furnished with a loadstone with which to place the nails. The school has its shop of prosthetic appliances where the ingenuity of the doctor seeks a solution to the most varied problems. As much care is bestowed upon the intellectual development of the pupils as upon their physical re-education.[1]

The Mayor of Lyons had determined on founding a similar school in his own town, when the world-war broke out, and turned his thoughts into other channels. It was then that he adapted the Charleroi methods to the re-education of the victims of the war, and he opened the first *School for the Wounded* at Lyons on 16 December, 1914. He entrusted its organisation and management to M. Basèque, the secretary of the Charleroi University of Labour. The collaboration of the Charleroi University is thus clearly shewn, and when M. Poincaré went over the Institution at Lyons, he was able to appreciate the first fruits of the fine co-operation between France and Belgium : some hundreds of those wounded in the war, those who have had an upper or a lower limb amputated, and those suffering from ankylosis, become gradually able to take up work again, thanks to the ingenious apparatus and systems for re-education, thought out by the technical staff of the institution.

The second *Industrial School for the wounded*

[1] Ed. Herriot, *L'Ecole des blessés.* Le Journal, Paris 23 Nov., 1914.

to be opened was that of Saint Maurice,
Paris.

It was again for Belgian collaboration that the
French applied when founding the third *Industrial
School for the Wounded,* which is that at Mont-
pellier. Its technical manager is M. Drousart,
General Secretary of the provincial schools for
technical instruction, in the town of Tournay.

Its Medical Director is Dr. Jeanbrau, Professor
of Medicine at Montpellier. The institution is
modelled upon that at Charleroi and amongst
its teachers is M. Tamenne of Charleroi, whose
right arm has been amputated, and who gives his
writing and educational courses with his left
hand   Specialists teach joinery, cabinet-making,
varnishing, wood - turning, plan - drawing, accountancy, short-hand, etc.

The schools at Lyons and Montpellier, organised
and directed by two Belgians, are institutions
which depend entirely upon the French Government, and are not supposed to admit any but French
pupils. Nevertheless, the Montpellier School
has a large contingent of Russian wounded,
and will shortly be admitting some Serbians
As to the Belgian wounded, they receive their
re-education at the *Belgian School at Post-Villez*
(Eure), which was opened in October, 1915.
This school, as well as the *Belgian Depôt for*

Invalids of the War at Saint Adresse, have been established by the Belgian Ministry of War, without the help of the technical education staff of Hainaut. The Charleroi school has, in each case, indirectly served as a model for all the schools for the wounded that have been founded in France since the war.

There is room to mention here the part taken by the Belgians in the invention of new prosthetic apparatus. These may be divided into two large groups : (1) Prosthetic Apparatus, for the lower limbs (peg-legs and artificial legs) ; (2) Prehensile apparatus (upper limbs).

Most interesting instruments have been invented by the Belgians for the lower limbs. Dr. Hendrickx, of the Rouen Hospital, and Dr. Martin, from the Depage Hospital at La Panne, have invented a wooden leg (on the American system), that is quite remarkable. We had the opportunity of seeing an exhibition of certain models at the Congress of the Allies for the study of industrial re-education, which was held in Paris at the *Grand Palais*, in May, 1917. The French Government was keenly interested in these appliances and approved the principle on which they were made. The Belgian army was the first to adopt the system of American artificial legs.

M. Drousart [1] had some prehensile appliances, which have given entire satisfaction, made at the Montpellier school, and these have been adopted by the Department of Public Health. They are issued to all those who have suffered amputation in the XVI district. One innovation is of great interest. The school has succeeded in teaching the wounded how to make these prosthetic appliances. This presents two undeniable advantages. (1) The number of specialists in this art had become quite insufficient since the necessities of the war had led to the invention of new orthopædic appliances ; it is, therefore, to a certain extent, a new craft that has arisen, and it was right that the victims of the war should, themselves, be the first to profit by it ; (2) The wounded soldiers, having themselves become the makers of the instruments, are most valuable advisers to those who invent the instruments that are to replace the missing or paralyzed limb.

We have thought it would be of interest to add this short notice of the working of the

[1] Ed. Drousart, *La ré éducation des mutilés de la guerre.* La Revue méridianate des Idées, Novembre, 1916, Montpellier ; *La perfectionnement des appareils orthopédiques pour re-education professionnelle.* Bulletin de l'œuvre des Mutilés de la guerre de la XVI région, 1st, Octobre, 1916, Montpellier. See also Dr. Jeanbrazz, *L'Ecole professionnelle des blessés de la XVI région a Montpellier.* Pamphlet 96 p., 1916. Montpellier.

Belgian methods of technical education ; at the very time when Charleroi was being bombarded by the enemy, its influence was shining across the world, its initiative was being associated with France in the great work of rescuing the men who had returned from the war ' incomplete,' and restoring them to work and to society.

THE END.